Employee Assistance Programs

COPYRIGHT ACKNOWLEDGMENTS

For Gary Fair, Sister Marie Veronica Janousek,
and Terry McGeeney

friends and mentors

and for all of my colleagues on staff at the ACCESS Employee
Assistance Program, Via Christi Regional Medical Center,
Wichita, Kansas. In alphabetical order, they are:

Vel Boudreaux

Cheri Darbe

Ray Novak

Jan Roberts

Al Schmidt

Dan Smarsh

Marvell Sosa

Ann Stewart

CONTENTS

INTRODUCTION

With the exception of two brief excursions into the alcohol and drug treatment field, I've worked in employee assistance since 1979. How I came to the field was entirely serendipitous; after teaching history at both the high school and university levels for 16 years, I decided I wanted to do something different but had no idea of what that might be. Shortly after leaving my last teaching assignment, I had the good fortune to meet an acquaintance who worked in employee assistance and suggested that I consider seeking employment in the field. Since I knew nothing about employee assistance, my first reactions to his suggestions were those of curiosity and skepticism. To make a long story short, I followed up on his suggestion, and to this day I'm grateful that I did.

I consider myself very fortunate. During my tenure in the field I have had the opportunity to meet a great many intelligent and creative people who are dedicated to their work and who contributed enormously to my appreciation of and respect for the uniqueness and potential of employee assistance. Anchored as it is in the worksite, it has a clearly defined context and the capacity to address many kinds of problems that would be difficult, if not impossible, to address in any other context. But there's the rub: As a colleague once put it, employee assistance has a great deal of "untapped potential," and he was precisely right—which raises the questions I hope to address in the following chapters. Why has employee assistance, especially within the past 10 to 15 years, so consistently fallen short of realizing that potential? The answer to that question may be found, partially at least, in the answer to another question: Why have some employee assistance professionals, wittingly or unwittingly, sacrificed the integrity of the field for short-term gain or the promise of influence? And, finally, a question of a different sort: What is the *essential* nature and purpose of employee assistance? With the exception of Paul Roman and a few others this last question is rarely asked anymore.

It was with these questions in mind and within this broad context that I began to formulate the ideas for this book. On the surface at least, the employee assistance field would seem to have matured. It now has professional journals, including the *EAP Digest, The Employee Assistance Quarterly,* and the *EAP Association Exchange,* all of which suggest a kind of coming of age for the field. Add to this the presence of two professional organizations, the Employee Assistance Professionals Association (EAPA), formerly the Association of Labor-Management Administrators and Consultants on Alcoholism (ALMACA), and the Employee Assistance Society of North America (EASNA), and it would seem that the professional circle is complete.

And, indeed, in many ways it is. Employee assistance is well known today among both human service professionals and business people; corporations of all kinds and sizes, as well as government agencies at all levels, have employee assistance programs. It is rare today to meet a business person who has not at least heard of employee assistance and rarer still to meet a mental health professional who is not familiar with employee assistance as both profession and career track. Formally, at least, employee assistance would appear to have arrived. It is recognized and recognizable, in possession of national certification (through EAPA), and enjoying the prestige that comes with a degree of legitimacy.

And yet, the field, far from being secure, is actually in a state of dissolution that is far advanced. It is my belief, based on my experience and the experience of others in the field, that employee assistance, as a profession and as a practical endeavor, is in serious trouble. For although it may be said to have arrived in some sense, it is far from certain that it will remain. There are several threats to the integrity of the field, and these have to do primarily with the attitudes and behaviors of employee assistance professionals themselves, some of whom seem bent on turning the field into a caricature of itself. Even a cursory review of the periodical literature in the field reveals a preoccupation with trendy but nebulous ideas, such as "change," and politically correct notions, such as multiculturalism and diversity. Then there is an exaggerated emphasis on professional prerogatives (all too often the bane of professional organizations) at the expense of fundamentals, and attempts to diminish the role of management in employee assistance programs (witness the present EAPA definition of employee assistance that makes no mention of management's indispensable role in anchoring employee assistance in the worksite. As we will see, there is a close connection between the profession's obsessive focus on professional prerogatives and management's disappearance from employee assistance programs, the most obvious instance of this being the profession's change in name from ALMACA to EAPA, which was a harbinger of things to come). All this and so far we have not even mentioned some of the more obvious distractions, such as managed mental health care, treatment modalities of one kind or another, clinical activities, and "super" EAPs.

Moreover, there is a great deal of talk about EAP "models," with some people suggesting that employee assistance can be anything one wishes to make it (even to mention the word "models," plural, suggests the depth of the problem and the confusion in the field). And then there are those who would like to see employee assistance shaped entirely by market forces. Although they overlap considerably, for the purpose of discussion I've divided the major threats to the field into three main categories: the supermen, the nihilists, and the centaurs.

In the first instance—that of the supermen—these are the people who would like to see employee assistance programs become involved in programs and functions such as work/life programs, welfare-to-work programs, and outplacement/retirement programs, among others, while still maintaining the core technology. But it is at least questionable whether employee assistance programs can assume these additional functions and still provide traditional employee assistance services to employers and employees, or whether the sheer multiplicity of these commitments will fragment and destroy the field. (An instructive and ominous parallel here is what has happened to our public schools during the last three to four decades when they tried to become all things to all people—from purveyors of sex education to gurus promoting the enhancement of self-esteem. In attempting to satisfy all sorts of discrepant and discordant demands they succeeded only in destroying the system.) Before we venture further in this direction, it might be well to develop specific criteria by which we can determine the suitability of certain kinds of activities for employee assistance.

Then there are the nihilists—those who would like to discard the entire traditional structure of employee assistance, including the core technology, often on the basis of no more than fad, whimsy, or expediency, and offer whatever services, largely unspecified, employers might request. Their desire is to abandon all standards and conventions.

Finally, there are the centaurs—those who in the past 15 years or so have been advocating the "integration" of employee assistance and managed mental health care. In books and numerous articles in the professional literature, they have made every effort to demonstrate and justify the advantages to be gained by integrating the two, suggesting even that integration will strengthen employee assistance. As we will see, their efforts have not only been less than convincing but defy common sense.

The book is divided into three parts and a conclusion. Part I is entitled "A Profession Adrift" and reviews the current state of employee assistance and the roots of the problems facing the field; Part II is entitled "In Search of Roots" and suggests why employee assistance, if it is to become once more a vital entity, must return to its traditional roots; Part III is entitled "Of Centaurs and Supermen" and maintains that the profession's current affiliation with managed mental health care has been disastrous for the field and that the profession's interest in developing super EAPs is also leading it away from its traditional activities; the Conclusion is entitled "Function and Authority" and provides both a summary of the main points of the book and a conceptual framework for addressing the issues of change and permanence.

What I hope to demonstrate in this book is the need for roots for employee assistance—roots that will enable the field to withstand pressures, both from within and without, to make it something that it is not and that it cannot be without losing its integrity. The following is from Simone Weil's *The Need for Roots*, and although Weil is writing about cultural rootedness in its broadest sense, the conceptual implications hold for specific institutions and their functions or purposes: *"To be rooted is perhaps the most important and least recognized need of the human soul. It is one of the hardest to define. A human being has roots by virtue of his real, active and natural participation in the life of a community which preserves in living shape certain particular treasures of the past and certain particular expectations for the future"* (41, italics added).

"Certain particular treasures of the past and certain particular expectations for the future" constitute the sum and substance of societies and institutions. Absent these treasures and expectations, that is to say, roots, societies and institutions perish or, at best, become merely pale imitations of what they were designed to be. But as Weil also suggests, it is the human being who, "by virtue of his real, active, and natural participation in the life of the community," gives form and substance to those treasures and expectations. It is the human being who is both the carrier and the substantive form of a culture.

Collectively, however, it is institutions, the "life of a community," that embody memory and hope, both of which are necessary if a community is to maintain any sense of direction. For an institution—any institution—comes into existence in response to a particular need. Although this may sound banal, it needs to be reasserted in view of the popularity of trends and fads such as deconstructionism, a pervasive moral relativism (and its twin, nihilism), increasingly higher levels of abstraction in language, and a kind of general obfuscation in communication.

Thus, an institution always serves a primary if not an exclusive purpose. Whether we are talking about an educational institution, the family, or a corporation, to cite just three, institutions respond to a need, and to the extent they are able to satisfy that need they remain functional, that is to say, they retain their authority. But when institutions lose sight of their primary purpose, that is, when they abandon their primary purpose or take on other or multiple functions, they dissipate their energies and fail to respond to the need that initially called them into existence. At that point they are moribund, and this is the point that employee assistance is fast approaching, if indeed it is not already there. All of this is but another way of saying that *there is a close, intimate, and irrevocable relationship between function and authority.*

My theses in this book are two: (1) *that over the course of the past 10 to 15 years employee assistance has been steadily retreating from the worksite, its only ground and the only context wherein it has any meaning or purpose, and that, as a result, the field is in danger of becoming extinct;* and (2) *that if the field is to recover its purpose and vitality, it will have to return to its roots.* For several reasons, all of which we will explore, employee assistance has been severed from its roots in the worksite, and the results have been no less than catastrophic. I also hope to demonstrate what will be necessary if the field is to recover its vitality, hence its authority. Writing in the March 1994 issue of *Employee Assistance*, Paul Roman, one of the most astute observers of the employee assistance field today, sums up the issues this way: "I worry because I am certain that much of what is practiced under the label of EA work does not bear the slightest resemblance to what most of us think should be there. As I have observed repeatedly . . . the field has no boundaries, and it easily surrenders its unique identity and assumes the form of clinical treatment" (11). As Roman suggests, it is the "unique identity" of the field that is at stake, for without that identity—an identity that is defined and circumscribed by the worksite—employee assistance, at least as we have known it, will cease to exist. Again, Roman: "*Without a steadfast focus on the integration of EA into the workplace,* and without better education of those workplace decision makers as to what they should expect when they implement an EA function, things will only get worse—a circumstance that will adversely affect the welfare of the entire EA community" (11, italics added). Put another way: It is the dynamics of human interaction in the worksite—not clinical activities or managed mental health care or any of the other currently fashionable ideologies—that constitute the proper and legitimate focus of employee assistance. For this reason, we will be returning again and again in this book to those two very basic ideas mentioned by Roman—integration and education.

Except perhaps indirectly, my approach in this essay will not be of the how-to-do-it variety. My focus will be essentially conceptual; what I hope to do is explore in some detail the essential conceptual structure of employee assistance, the sine qua non, as it were, of employee assistance, at least as I understand it, and to lay bare the roots of the field, roots that, I believe, cannot be discarded without permanent and irrevocable damage to the field. Thus my efforts will be restricted in scope, conceptual in nature, and limited to those elements that are essential to employee assistance.

I am deeply indebted to colleagues in the field, past and present, who were and in a very real sense remain my mentors. Bob Francoeur and Stan Dole were the first to introduce me to the field of employee assistance in 1979. Then there are latter day colleagues, notably Vel Boudreaux, Cheri Darbe, Gary Fair, Sister Marie Veronica Janousek CSJ, Rita Loveys, Terry McGeeney, Sid Miller, Gary Morgan (now deceased), Ray Novak, Jan Roberts, Al Schmidt, Dan Smarsh, Marvell Sosa, Ann Stewart, and Martha Webb. To all of these good people, from whom I've learned and continue to learn a great deal, I owe an enormous debt of gratitude.

I am also greatly indebted to Paul Roman, whose writings on employee assistance continue to provoke me and on more than one occasion compelled me to rethink my own beliefs about the nature and purpose of employee assistance. As the reader will note, my debt to him is indicated in the following pages by my liberal use of excerpts from his work.

Last, but very far from being least, I would like to express my gratitude to the good people of Via Christi Regional Medical Center, Wichita, Kansas, for the unparalleled opportunity to work in an environment permeated by a strong sense of mission, which is to say, of loving concern for others. Had I written the script myself, I could not have described a better place to work. I should also note that our employee assistance program is under the division of Mission Services where, in my judgment, all hospital-based employee assistance programs should be. All of which tends to disprove, in this case at least, the old adage that you can't have it all.

Part I

A PROFESSION ADRIFT

Chapter 1

THE CURRENT STATE OF EMPLOYEE ASSISTANCE

Those who are familiar with employee assistance know that the field is changing, and they know also that the changes, or at least some of them, are marked by controversy and confusion. For some, the changes are necessary and even welcome. Taking the broadest possible view, they suggest that over the past half century or so American society and especially the economy have changed beyond recognition and that employee assistance, if it wishes to remain relevant and effective in the new environment, must change also. They point to developments such as globalization, the presence of women, minorities, and the handicapped in the workplace, extraordinary technological innovation, and the increasing cultural diversity to be found in society and the workplace. Although these do not exhaust the range of changes that have taken place and continue to take place in our society and economy, they are, so it is argued, among the most important and describe a far different world from the one into which employee assistance was born over a half century ago.

But this is only half of the equation. The other half centers specifically on how employee assistance has functioned in the past and whether it can continue to function in that manner in the future. And this is where the controversy and confusion arise. If the assumption is that employee assistance must change to meet changing conditions, how should it change, and what should it change? Is the Core Technology (which will be discussed in some detail in Part II), that mainstay, in theory at least, of employee assistance practice still relevant, or is it, because of its single-minded focus on the worksite, no more than a relic and an obstacle to dealing competently with the challenges facing employee assistance today, especially those that have to do with reducing or containing the increasing costs of health care, especially mental health care? Implicit in that question is another: Should employee assistance today focus on behavioral health care rather than behavioral risk management, as it has done in the past? And what about the emergence of managed mental health care and efforts to integrate it and employee assistance? Can employee assistance, in other words, stand alone and remain effective, or must it become an integral part of hybrid behavioral and managed mental health care systems and in the process lose its distinct identity and functions, as some maintain will happen with integration?

For many people in the field, however, these questions are moot; questions as to the nature and purpose of employee assistance and how it will function in the future have, they maintain, already been decided by the market, and the only remaining relevant issue is the occurrence of ethical improprieties in those employee assistance programs that are components of behavioral or managed mental health care programs. This is the position taken by David A. Sharar and William L. White in two articles in recent issues of the *EAP Association Exchange* (hereinafter the *Exchange*). Unlike much of what appears in the *Exchange,* these articles are substantive and informative and address an issue that is of the greatest importance for the future of employee assistance. Moreover—and this is the great merit of both articles—the authors frame the discussion within a context that is ethical rather than merely technical. The importance of this last point cannot be overemphasized, for if we are to understand what is happening in employee assistance today, we must understand it as first and foremost an ethical problem of major significance for the field, and one that has major implications for the future as well.

The first of the two articles is entitled "Referrals and Ownership Structures" and appeared in the September/October 2001 issue of the *Exchange* with a thematic subtitle that describes the article: "The first of two articles on the need for a revised ethic in employee assistance considers whether ownership structures can improperly influence EAP professionals" (14–15). The second article, entitled "EAP Competence and Value," appeared in the November/December 2001 issue of the *Exchange* with a descriptive subtitle: "The second of two articles on the need for a revised ethic in employee assistance addresses concerns about the use of subcontractors by national EAP vendors" (14–15). The articles complement one another and, as the authors tell us, grew out of a recent study that "examined how a random sample of employee assistance professionals perceive the state of ethical conduct related to business practices within the EA/managed behavioral health care field." They also tell us that "[t]wenty-two percent of survey respondents identified the ethics of EA referrals as among the most important or critical business ethical issues facing the industry." Since these articles examine an issue of the greatest importance for employee assistance and are all too rare in the literature, we will summarize the contents primarily in the authors' own words and reserve commentary for the last. We will review the articles in the order in which they appeared in the *Exchange*.

Sharar and White state that "[m]any survey respondents expressed concern that parent organizations [defined as behavioral health agencies, hospitals, or private clinics] that own and operate EAPs expect them to generate treatment revenue via a pattern of preferential referral to vested programs or practitioners. According to these respondents, the parent implicitly or explicitly uses its EAP division or department as a business development strategy for the expansion of 'feeder' systems and increased market security." And herein lies the ethical problem facing these kinds of EAPs: "Given that an 'objective' or 'neutral' referral is a 'cornerstone of an ethical EAP' (EASNA Code of Ethics), an expectation of preferential referrals would create conflicting loyalties for the EA professional, potentially undermining his/her fundamental obligation to serve as a client advocate. An incentive would exist for the EA professional to base referrals on financial interests that conflict with 'neutral' or 'objective' assessments of how and/or where a client's treatment needs can best be met."

The authors then ask the obvious question: "Are there ethically acceptable ways for EA professionals to refer clients to other practitioners or programs within their own organization?," and state that, in fact, there are. They cite several, all of them suggested by survey respondents themselves as ways of mitigating "any appearance or accusation of unethical conduct":

- Fully disclosing (to both employer and client) any affiliation with proposed referral options;
- Offering an "objective" presentation of more than one referral option to the client;
- Providing clinical justification that the referral is in the best interests of the client;

- Refusing to accept any direct gain or financial remuneration for referring clients;

- Instituting a peer review program to monitor and evaluate the quality and appropriateness of referrals; and

- Developing a utilization/service summary report for employers containing detailed information on patterns of referral for continuing care and treatment.

Under a subheading entitled "Ownership Structure Conflicts," Sharar and White state: "In theory, the predominant ownership structures among EAPs are set up to encourage referrals for treatment to affiliated programs to generate revenue (e.g., EAPs owned by parent organizations) or to discourage referral for treatment to minimize costs (e.g., EAPs owned by national insurance or managed care companies). Organizational financial strategies that induce EA professionals to either limit necessary care or encourage unnecessary care have the potential to conflict with the welfare of the individual client or the interests of the client organization." In the next paragraph, the authors tell us that "[e]thical problems are more likely when owners encourage certain decisions or referrals by financially rewarding or penalizing EA professionals or gatekeepers on the basis of their pattern of practice." They conclude this section of the article by stating that "[w]e must encourage employers to select EAP vendors and models that foster the principled practice of EA programming."

Under the last subheading in the article, which is entitled "A New Professional Ethic?," Sharar and White state that "[t]hese are challenging times for the EA field. We perceive a growing disconnect between the historic concept of employee assistance ethics and the changing circumstances and emerging environment in the provision of employee assistance services. The current climate of intense competition for increased market share, operating losses, 'merger mania,' referral incentives masked as integrated delivery systems, and the blurring of boundaries between EA entities and ancillary products is unlikely to foster an atmosphere that nurtures high standards in referral and business practices."

It is also the case, as the authors suggest, that "the EA field is being pulled in one direction by members of the traditional guard, who rail against programs they feel have drifted away from the original mission of employee assistance, and in another by programs and entrepreneurs that are diverse, expansive, and market- or profit-driven. The latter are calling for a new professional ethic that takes into account a broader, more complex set of business ethical guidelines and responsibilities."

Accordingly, the authors call for a revision of "our codes of ethics and conduct," and suggest that "the leadership of the employee assistance field . . . engage in ethics-related advocacy by organizing and supporting an 'ethics summit' composed of a cross-section of EA leaders, professionals, constituents (employee/employer clients), and representatives from allied fields (e.g., human resources, benefits, labor, managed care, treatment, and so on). This summit would be a working meeting, with subgroups entering into a dialogue on how to revise the field's ethics codes to be more relevant and informative in the area of business ethics. Another goal of the summit could be to explore ways to develop an independent audit function for all external EAPs."

The second article, as I noted above, is entitled "EAP Competence and Value" and appeared in the November/December 2001 issue of the *Exchange*. Essentially, it recapitulates the basic themes of the first article, but the authors do emphasize at least two other important areas of concern. The first of these is "[a] broader ethical concern among survey respondents" who perceive a "decline in the quality of EA programming in the face of massive consolidation and large-scale national mergers." The authors state that "[a]t the heart of this concern is a perception that national vendors lack, as a core value, a collaborative, community-based ethos based on geographic proximity, personal communication, community benefit, and outcome rather than cost. This lack of an ethos manifests itself in ways that minimize some of the potential strengths of local/regional EA firms," such as the fact that generally the latter have intimate knowledge of their communities and are able to respond more quickly to the needs and concerns of employers. On the other hand, "[n]ational EA vendors . . . claim to offer many program features and support capabilities that are especially attractive to large employers with multiple locations," such as superior resources and "[e]conomies of scale—and, ultimately, more competitive prices—that are unattainable in local/regional models." The same holds true for "subsets of national vendors" who "have 'regionally-based' account management and service center sites that emphasize local integration, coordination and responsiveness."

Finally, Sharar and White state that "[t]he reality is that work organizations, as purchasers of EAPs, ultimately determine what constitutes a quality program. Decisions about whether an EAP provider will be local or national in scope, for profit or nonprofit, or owned by a parent organization or managed care company are made largely in response to employers' needs and preferences."

As I stated earlier, both of these articles are substantive and informative; they are also timely in that the processes they describe—"intense competition for increased market share, operating losses, 'merger mania,' referral incentives masked as integrated delivery systems, and the blurring of boundaries between EA entities and ancillary products"—are accelerating and show no signs of slowing down, which will indeed make it difficult "to foster an atmosphere that nurtures high standards in referral and business practices." I would hope also that the articles spark a more vigorous debate—at least more vigorous than what we've seen so far—among employee assistance professionals, including the leadership of the profession. Having said all that, and unreservedly commending the authors for their courage and perspicuity in addressing issues that have the most profound significance for employee assistance and that for far too long have been ignored by the profession, I must, however, submit that both articles are seriously flawed. Indeed, they are conceptually incoherent and will, ultimately, probably be more confusing than enlightening, for three reasons. First, what Sharar and White are describing is not employee assistance, at least not employee assistance as it is defined and described by the Core Technology, but rather a kind of gatekeeping function or mechanism, which is designed, as they themselves suggest, to deny or restrict necessary services or to channel people into treatment programs of one kind or another, often unnecessarily. Nowhere in their articles is there any mention of the indispensable relationship between employee assistance and the worksite or how those employee assistance programs, which are components of integrated delivery systems, can function *as* employee assistance programs when they are no more than gatekeepers for systems whose imperatives dictate their activities. Nor is there any mention of traditional employee assistance concepts such as the "troubled employee," "productivity," or "constructive confrontation," among others, all of which we will have occasion to review in subsequent pages. When Sharar and White speak of employee assistance they describe it as a health care delivery system or, at least, a component of integrated behavioral or managed mental health care systems that have little or no interest in the worksite or in any other aspect of traditional EAP programming. Moreover—and this is perhaps the most conceptually incoherent aspect of their articles—they seem to believe that there is nothing inherently wrong or remiss or unethical, or even potentially unethical, in integrated delivery systems that a code of ethics might not fix. But it must be kept in mind that employee assistance is not, nor was it ever intended to be, a health care delivery system or a component of the latter; its purpose was and is that of behavioral risk management, and it is precisely this—the effort to make employee assistance something that it was never intended to be—that is the source of the ethical problems. Employee assistance was born in the worksite, nurtured by the worksite, and had its essential features framed by the worksite, and it is its relationship to the worksite that is the only conceptual framework within which we can begin to understand employee assistance. Its primary focus is productivity, not mental health care, and the supervisor's office, not the therapist's office. Remove employee assistance from the worksite—as Sharar, White, and a host of others are attempting to do—and it is no longer employee assistance. Whenever we attempt to make an entity serve a purpose other than that for which it was designed, we will have improprieties that, if not ethical in nature, will create a great deal of confusion. This brings us to our second point.

Like so many articles and books that excel in describing particular and concrete problems in very understandable ways but fail miserably when it comes to proposing specific solutions for those problems, or veer off into a rootless abstraction, which at first glance seems imposing but ultimately tells us little or nothing about how we can correct those problems, Sharar and White tell us what they believe might be the solution for unethical behavior in behavioral and managed mental health care systems, namely, an "ethics summit." And this is perhaps the most otherworldly aspect of their articles. Are they suggesting that the people who own and operate these systems do not know the difference between right and wrong, or that they do but are driven primarily by the imperatives of these systems with little or no concern for the consequences? If the former, we are indeed in a bad way, and if the latter, an ethics summit will do little more than produce more talk about ethics. The authors would have been on more solid ground if they had addressed the issue of the essential incompatibility of employee assistance and integrated health care delivery systems, but then this would have changed the entire tenor and thesis of their articles. The fundamental issue is whether employee assistance programs can become components of integrated health care delivery systems, a "revised" or "new professional ethic" notwithstanding, or whether there is an essential incompatibility between the two programs, and that, therefore, attempts to integrate them will not only distort the nature and purpose of employee assistance but will create insoluble problems for the latter. That the authors are at least aware of the problem is suggested when they state that two of the major reasons why there is so much confusion and controversy in the field are those of "referral systems masked as integrated delivery systems" and the "blurring of boundaries between EA entities and ancillary products," both of which are "unlikely to foster an atmosphere that nurtures high standards in referral and business practices." Indeed, these may be the most important insights in their articles, and they are precisely right; "referral systems masked as integrated delivery systems" and the "blurring of boundaries between EA entities and ancillary products" are inextricably intertwined—the latter leads inevitably to the former—and are the source of the ethical confusion in the field. What is perhaps most puzzling in this instance is that Sharar and White, rather than exploring this issue in some detail, simply pass it off to an "ethics summit," as if the latter will be able to resolve a problem that has its source in the very nature of the integrated delivery systems they seem to espouse. Perhaps another way of saying this is that an employee assistance program will be an employee assistance program or it will not. By virtue of the structure and purpose of employee assistance, it cannot function at one and the same time as employee assistance and as a gatekeeper or screening device for integrated behavioral or managed mental health care systems. It will be one or the other, but not both. Moreover, what is a "new professional ethic"? What would it look like? And what does "a broader, more complex set of business-related ethical guidelines and responsibilities" mean? Whence would come this new professional ethic? From what would it be derived? Would it be derived from the expectations and ambitions of the "programs and entrepreneurs that are diverse, expansive, and market- or profit-driven"? Or would it be derived from something that is external to those "programs and entrepreneurs," something that is objective in nature and applicable to any number of different situations where the potential for ethical impropriety is great? If the former, then we are saying no more than that the imperatives of these integrated delivery systems will dictate the code of ethics, which in turn will be used to justify the activities of these systems. This is not only circular reasoning, but by the very nature of that reasoning a whole host of other ethical questions are raised. If the latter, then we do not need an ethics summit; the nature and applicability of ethical systems have been the province of philosophers and theologians for thousands of years. Codes of ethics have only two sources: immanence and transcendence; if codes of ethics are immanent, they are derived from the position or field of discourse under consideration, and if transcendent, they are derived from something that is external to that position or field of discourse and are, therefore, objective in nature. I am not aware of any other sources for codes of ethics.

Also, what do Sharar and White mean when they call for an ethics summit to begin "a dialogue on how to revise the field's ethics codes to be more relevant and informative in the area of business ethics"? Are they suggesting that there are different kinds of ethics, including one just for business? And what does "relevant" mean? And when they state that they "perceive a growing disconnect between the historic concept of employee assistance ethics and the changing circumstances and emerging environment in the provision of employee assistance services," are they suggesting that employee assistance change its principles and practice to accommodate "changing circumstances" and the "emerging environment"? Or are they, implicitly at least, suggesting that employee assistance, governed as it is (or should be) by the Core Technology, is essentially incompatible with integrated health care delivery systems? This sentence is not at all clear.

If we are to understand employee assistance, we must begin at the beginning and ask: What is employee assistance? What is its essential nature and purpose? What is it designed to do? We will attempt to answer these questions in subsequent pages, but for the moment it is enough to note that Sharar and White do not address these questions, which is a major flaw in their articles. That the authors are aware of the limitations of ethics summits is indicated in the last paragraph of the first article where they cite a statement by Leon Kass: "Though originally intended to improve our deeds, the reigning practice in ethics, if truth be told, has, at best, improved our speech." Kass's point is well taken: We don't need more talk about ethics; what we need is ethical behavior.

Before we turn to our third and last point, two other issues raised by Sharar and White need to be addressed. While it is true that there is a "traditional guard" in the employee assistance field that believes that employee assistance has "drifted away from its original mission," the members of this group do not base their objections on nostalgia or some kind of misguided reverence for the past but on what they believe to be the abrogation of traditional and essential employee assistance principles and practice by programs and entrepreneurs that have little or no interest in employee assistance as such. Their concern, in other words, is for the integrity of employee assistance as it is defined by the Core Technology. The second issue is the makeup or composition of the ethics summit advocated by Sharar and White; noticeably absent from the summit are those whose business it is to understand ethics and provide ethical guidelines for human behavior, namely, philosophers and theologians.

Finally, there is the issue of who decides what a quality program is. For the authors, "[t]he reality is that work organizations, as purchasers of EAPs, ultimately determine what constitutes a quality program. Decisions about whether an EAP provider will be local or national in scope, for profit or nonprofit, or owned by a parent organization or managed care company are made largely in response to employers' needs and preferences." But do they? And are they? Is it the case that work organizations determine what constitutes a quality program? And if they do, upon what basis—and using what criteria—do they make those determinations? Are decisions of this sort made largely in response to employers' needs and preferences? Or are they driven by the imperatives of health care vendors, imperatives that constitute the very nature of integrated delivery systems? The answers to these questions are not at all as certain as the authors suggest. Indeed, one could easily make the case that if employers and work organizations are making these decisions they are doing so only in a formal, not in any substantive, sense. Moreover, are work organizations, as purchasers of EAPs, in fact purchasing EAPs, or are they purchasing integrated delivery systems of which the EAP is only one small and inconsequential part in the long-term plans and goals of these systems? Then there is what is perhaps the most important question of all, a question that we shall have occasion to ask again: Should the market, that is, work organizations, determine what constitutes a quality program, or should it be the employee assistance professional who makes that determination? The answer to that question will, in large part, determine the future of employee assistance.

Perhaps the most revealing aspect of these two articles—one that I'm sure was not intended by the authors—is the degree to which we as a culture have lost our ethical moorings. That Sharar and White deem it important to call for an ethics summit to "dialogue" on very basic issues of right and wrong is in and of itself remarkable. Is it the case that after several thousand years of civilization we still don't know the difference between right and wrong? Are codes of ethics relevant only to time, place, and circumstance; are they, in other words, no more than a kind of situation ethics that changes when the environment and circumstances change? Or is it the case that traditional codes of ethics are no longer valid in our brave new world? The recent travails of Enron, WorldCom, and Xerox are indeed disturbing, but they are merely symptomatic of a much broader and deeper ethical malaise in our society.

Perhaps the best critique of the authors' articles is in a letter to the editor in the March/April 2002 issue of the *Exchange*, entitled "Committed to Our Core Values." The author of the letter, Jeff Christie, puts it this way: "Regarding the recent set of articles by Messrs. Sharar and White, I would like to comment that codes of conduct are not designed to be malleable to the ever-changing world of 'product' delivery and financial structures. To the contrary, it is the very reality of this transient landscape that compels us to remain aware of, and committed to, our core ethical values. It's not the foot that should fit the shoe" (7). Just so.

If it isn't already obvious, I wish to make clear that my sympathies are with those—the "traditional guard"—who believe that employee assistance is in serious trouble. Altogether, I've worked in the field for some twenty years and thoroughly enjoy my work, but I've reached a point—indeed, I've been at that point for some time now—where I'm not always sure of what people mean when they talk about employee assistance. This makes me one of the naysayers; I believe, with William F. Buckley, Jr., that the purpose of a conservative—in this case an employee assistance conservative—is to stand athwart history and say "stop." I believe that employee assistance has lost all sense of purpose and direction and that its practitioners generally, and the leadership in particular, have no idea of where it's going or what it will do when it gets there. The field no longer has boundaries of any kind or a core set of principles, and no one, as far as I know, has been able to determine the nature of whatever kind of metamorphosis is taking place or where it is leading. I have no idea of what employee assistance is—at least as it is described by EAPA (Employee Assistance Professionals Association), the largest and most influential of the professional organizations in the field—or where it is going. Is it managed mental health care? Is it clinical activities, with the *DSM IV (Diagnostic and Statistical Manual of Mental Disorders IV)* taking center stage? Is it substance abuse treatment? Is it a kind of omnibus ideology designed to embrace and justify every fad or trendy movement that comes down the pike? Or is it something else—perhaps some combination of elements that dares not or, perhaps, cannot speak its name? I don't know, and it's clear that no one in EAPA's leadership knows either.

That this is not mere hyperbole or unwarranted criticism will be clear to anyone—anyone, that is, who has any knowledge of what employee assistance is or should be—who reads the *Exchange*. The *Exchange* describes itself as "The Magazine of the Employee Assistance Professionals Association" and is published every two months or six times a year. It is, in other words, the official mouthpiece of the association, and one would expect—or at least hope—that it would devote most of its pages to what employee assistance is and what it is not. But, alas, such is not the case; indeed, it is rare to find much of anything that is even remotely reminiscent of what employee assistance practitioners used to talk about, such as supervisor training, constructive confrontation, the Core Technology (that is occasionally mentioned in passing), policy statements, productivity, the troubled employee, and so on. These, it seems, have been relegated to the back burner.

To make my concerns somewhat more explicit, I've chosen some of the contents of recent issues of the *Exchange,* beginning with the March/April 2001 issue, which is appropriate since its focus is the profession's thirtieth anniversary. The cover is inscribed with the words "The Impact of EAPs," and this apparently is intended to be both hortatory and celebratory as well as the theme for the contents.

Under the heading "Front Desk," the first essay in this issue is by John Maynard and is entitled "The Next 30 Years." Maynard, who is cited as the chairman of EAPA's Advisory Committee, opens the essay with a question that sets the theme for his remarks: "What do the next 30 years hold for EAPs and EA professionals?" (2). The second paragraph provides a brief history of employee assistance culminating in a change of the profession's name from ALMACA (Association of Labor-Management Administrators and Consultants on Alcoholism) to EAPA in the late 1980s. Maynard states that "[b]y 1987, the field had grown and changed so much that the name of the association no longer reflected its full scope, so ALMACA became EAPA." In paragraph three he cites some of the specific changes the profession has witnessed during the last thirty years, including the growth of the profession's membership "from its 18 founding members" to "nearly 7,000 men and women in more than 20 countries." He also mentions some specific services that EAPs have added to their professional repertoire, "ranging from critical incident stress debriefings to work/life initiatives to legal and financial assistance, all within the framework of workplace-based core technology and program definition established and supported by EAPA." He concludes paragraph three with a few words about the certification process that, he states, "has raised the level of professionalism within our field."

Paragraph four continues the litany, this time with emphasis on trends in the workplace. Here he cites women and minorities in the workplace, workers who have child and elder care responsibilities, innovations in communications technology, and globalization, and suggests that these have changed the face of the workforce and by implication the way in which employee assistance will have to carry out its mission.

But there are problems here, and Maynard's statements are more conducive to skepticism than they are to admiration for the profession. Like much of the literature in the employee assistance field—especially in the *Exchange*—Maynard's essay is no more than an exercise in self-congratulatory adulation. For example, it offers neither evidence nor logic to support the notion that "the field had grown and changed so much" that it was necessary or even prudential to change the name of the profession from ALMACA to EAPA. If these are the changes Maynard is referring to as legitimation or justification for the change of name—and I presume they are—then he is engaging in mere assertion. Neither individually nor collectively do these developments suggest either empirically or logically any necessity for changing the name of the professional organization. In fact, one could easily argue—and we will do so in subsequent pages—that the change of name served only to narrow the scope and vision of the profession by isolating it from the broader community suggested by the name ALMACA. The best proof of that assertion is to be found in a recent letter dated September 10, 2001, from Linda Sturdivant (EAPA's president) to EAPA members informing them of the United Auto Workers (UAW) decision to end funding of individual memberships in EAPA, and one of the reasons cited by Sturdivant for the UAW's decision is "the change in the association's name (from ALMACA to EAPA)." Obviously not everyone is enamored of Maynard's notions of growth and change. We will review Sturdivant's letter in more detail in subsequent pages.

Equally disturbing, Maynard makes no mention of EAPA's acquiescence to the demands of the managed mental health care industry, which, along with the change of the profession's name, set the profession on a course that has been destructive of its heritage and principles. One could easily argue—and we will do so in Part III—that it would have been much more difficult for the managed mental health care industry to assume control of employee assistance had the profession maintained its ties with labor and management. Once those ties were severed, the profession was not only left defenseless against the pretensions of managed mental health care but it was forced to retreat from the only context that can provide it with structure and purpose—the worksite. For the behavioral or managed mental health care industry has no interest in the worksite, the troubled employee, productivity, or organizational development. Its only interest—its exclusive interest—is in controlling the costs associated with mental health care and the profits entailed in doing so.

That my concerns about managed mental health care and its effects on employee assistance are not merely idiosyncratic personal ones is borne out in a letter to the editor in the November/December 2000 issue of the *Exchange*. Aptly entitled "Absence of Clarity," the letter, authored by Mark Cohen, raises questions about the intent and purpose of an article published in the *Exchange* for May/June 2000. As Cohen, who is obviously well versed in the principles and practice of employee assistance, puts it: "The article describes the Shands Healthcare Program as an integrated EAP/behavioral health service, but never identifies its mission as that of an EAP; it only uses the term. This program, while it may be useful and worthwhile, actually describes a mental health benefit and not a program designed to improve job functioning" (3). Cohen follows these statements with a series of questions, all of them pertinent and to the point: "Does publishing this article mean that EAPA now accepts a definition of EAPs designed by insurance companies, HMOs, and behavioral health care organizations? Have we more than one definition of an EAP, and have we abandoned the responsibility to educate potential customers as to what an EAP is (and is not) and what behavioral health care is (and is not)? And what is EAPA's responsibility to keep our own members accurately informed?" In the last paragraph of his letter Cohen makes a point that Maynard and others in EAPA's leadership would do well to read and ponder frequently: "If EA professionals are to be recognized, appreciated, and sought out as having a defined area of expertise and a valued role in contributing to the resolution of workplace problems, then EAPA must lead the way by clarifying the public's perception of our mission." The key words in this last sentence are "having a defined area of expertise and a valued role in contributing to the resolution of workplace problems." But EAPA long ago abandoned the idea of an area of expertise, and in its fascination with all sorts of trendy notions, including managed mental health care, abandoned the idea of employee assistance as a means of resolving workplace problems. Nor does clarification of the principles and practice of employee assistance seem to be very high on EAPA's list of things to do.

The key to making sense—any kind of sense—of Maynard's essay is his use of the word "change." We have already mentioned his use of the word "changed" to justify the change of the profession's name from ALMACA to EAPA, and in paragraph five of his essay he again mentions "change." "We . . . can expect that the places we work, the services we provide, and the employers and employees we serve will change, perhaps dramatically. And we can expect that employee assistance will still be needed and practiced, though in what manner and by whom remain to be determined." The first of these two sentences is unremarkable—it merely reiterates the theme of his essay—but the second should be a wake-up call to those who believe in the importance of principles or standards. To suggest that we do not know how employee assistance will be practiced in the future or by whom is to suggest that it can be anything one wishes to make it. This in essence is the doctrine of nihilism, the belief that there is no such thing as objective truth, either intellectual or moral, and it is all premised on the vague notion of change.

Unfortunately, as we will see, Maynard is not alone in his careless use of the word change. Such usage permeates the human services field and the social sciences generally. It has become a kind of mantra and a warrant for issuing imprimaturs to all sorts of trendy notions. Seldom is the word described, defined, or explained in any particular or concrete way. It is simply assumed that change means progress, and anyone who might voice an objection to that equation is dismissed as reactionary or hopelessly out of touch with reality. It is also assumed that our modern age is a vast improvement on what has gone before, that we are in possession of a wisdom denied our ancestors, and that all that is necessary to effect change is ritual incantation that equates change with progress. One quick look at the history of the twentieth century should be enough to disabuse anyone of the notion that change always means progress.

Why, then, is there so much unqualified enthusiasm for change in so many quarters of our society? First, and perhaps most obvious, we tend, consciously or unconsciously, to equate change with technological innovation and the latter in turn with progress. And although it is quite legitimate, in some instances at least, to equate technological change with progress, it is not at all legitimate to equate every instance or every kind of change with progress. Change is not a synonym for progress; indeed, change can just as easily mean regression as well as progression. Second, ours is an unprincipled and standardless society, by which I mean that we are heavily invested in the doctrines of cultural and moral relativism. The notion that one idea, opinion, or cultural form is as valid as any other and that none has a right to claim primacy has its source in the absence of standards and principles that would enable us to form judgments, evaluate events, or make discriminations. The upshot of this is that we cannot reject even the most pernicious of influences, for to do so would imply the presence of standards or principles, which are anathema to the modern mind. We are reminded here of Sharar and White's concerns about the ethical behavior in much of what passes for employee assistance today. Third, the notion that change means progress is a convenient way to circumvent the thinking process and deny the nature of reality. Perhaps another way of saying this is that the word change has become a kind of abstract "standard" or "principle" by which we can gather up all of the contradictions, anomalies, and pluralities of life, dissolve them in a kind of ethereal fog, and then claim that this is the best of all possible worlds.

The next essay in the March/April 2001 issue of the *Exchange* is by Linda Sturdivant, EAPA's president, and is entitled "Taking Concrete

Steps." Like Maynard's essay, Sturdivant's is future-oriented but as the title of her essay suggests, it is in a somewhat more specific way. She mentions the U.S. Department of Transportation's new regulations on alcohol and drug testing, several conferences and training programs, the establishment of "the EAPA Professional Development Institute, a new initiative designed to assess members' educational needs and develop and conduct training programs to meet those needs," and the EAPA Board of Directors' strategic plan. At the heart of her essay, however, is the latter—the "strategic plan"—which, according to Sturdivant, includes "expanding and improving our Web site, creating new communications tools to keep members better informed of developments within our association and profession, and acquiring and developing new products for our Resource Center," all of which, she believes, "will increase the level of services and benefits to EAPA members and add value to membership in our association" (4–5).

No one, I believe, would quarrel with the goals outlined above. They are entirely proper and even necessary if the profession is to keep its members informed of developments in the field. But it is the next paragraph that should raise red flags, for in addition to the programs, initiatives, and training sessions Sturdivant mentions, she also mentions something called "strategic alliances," which are part of the strategic plan. "The strategic plan also calls for EAPA to establish 'strategic alliances' with employers, unions, insurance carriers, state and local governments, colleges and universities, other employee assistance groups, and organizations in EA-related fields such as human resources and work/life programming. This process includes attending meetings, workshops, and conferences on mental health, substance abuse, child and elder care, and dozens of other issues that affect workforce productivity." She also states that "[o]ne of our most important alliances is with the U.S. Congress, which in the 2001–2002 session is expected to consider legislation that would provide equal access to substance abuse treatment."

EAPA's "strategic alliances," at least as Sturdivant describes them, are ambitious. Another word to describe them would be grandiose. Moreover, one is entitled to ask the obvious question: What do all of these strategic alliances have to do with employee assistance? What is their purpose? Other than the vague phrase, "issues that affect workplace productivity," Sturdivant tells us nothing about means and ends. And did not the profession at one time have an alliance—strategic or otherwise—with labor and management? And was not that alliance called ALMACA?

Sturdivant is not at all clear about the purposes, ends, or objectives of these alliances; specifically, what are they designed to do? Second, Sturdivant's use of the words "strategic alliances" suggests that her primary interest is power, not employee assistance. Third, and most important, Sturdivant's essay indicates the degree to which EAPA's leadership has lost contact with employee assistance *as* employee assistance. Her desire to form an "alliance" with Congress—for any reason—suggests the seduction of power. Is it a purpose of employee assistance to lobby Congress? This is the language of the would-be power broker, not the language of the employee assistance professional.

Instead of grandiose schemes to enhance the power and prestige of EAPA, Sturdivant would be well advised, especially in her capacity as president of the association, to focus on the problems—many of them serious—plaguing the field today (witness the UAW's refusal to continue funding individual memberships in EAPA). Indeed, many of these problems stem from the leadership's preoccupation with the trendy, the irrelevant, and the spurious. EAPA's and Sturdivant's approach to employee assistance is an all too common one today, especially in the human services field—where the focus is on the ephemeral, where, in other words, principle is sacrificed in the interests of power, status, and prestige.

The March/April 2002 issue of the *Exchange* also raises several important issues and questions. On the cover is the question "What are EAPs?" Replies from several writers constitute the major theme of this particular issue. In a foreword to the articles in this section, the editors state the following: "[W]hat, exactly, are EAPs, and what services do they provide? The answers, it seems, differ from workplace to workplace. Ironically, as EAPs have become more and more popular they have become less and less understood, providing services that employers say are useful but cannot clearly identify or quantify." They conclude their forward with the following: "What are EAPs? Perhaps the better question to ask is: 'What will EAPs look like three decades from now?' The answer to that question depends on what EAPs do, and don't do, today." The first thing to note is that the question is not "What is an employee assistance program?" or "What is employee assistance?," but "What are EAPs?," suggesting, implicitly at least, that there may be several different kinds of employee assistance programs or that employee assistance may take different forms, which in turn may suggest why employers "cannot clearly identify or quantify" exactly what an employee assistance program is. Thus, right from the beginning the editors muddy the waters, first, by asking the question—"What are EAPs?"—which is the wrong question, and, second, by asking the question—"What will EAPs look like three decades from now?"—which is no more than a way of avoiding coming to terms with the nature and purpose of employee assistance. If this were not enough, the editors then cloud the issue even more by suggesting that the answer to this last question "depends on what EAPs do, and don't do, today"—a response that in a narrow technical sense is accurate but within the context of the foreword is meaningless. Although it appears to be lost on the editors, this is precisely the kind of thinking that is conducive to confusion on the part of employers. The editors' inability or unwillingness to state exactly what employee assistance is and is not is a certain guarantee that employers will remain confused and employee assistance "less and less understood."

This issue of the *Exchange,* as well as others, goes a long way, I believe, towards explaining the confusion in the employee assistance field today. To make these remarks somewhat more specific, we will review several of the articles in this section of the March/April 2002 issue of the *Exchange.*

One of the more substantive articles is by Brenda R. Blair and is entitled "Consultative Services: Providing Added Value to Employers." Blair addresses the problems in the field directly by listing the reasons why in her opinion there is a great deal of confusion, especially among employers, as to what employee assistance is. She states that "for many EAPs, the focus on individuals has been paired with a decreased emphasis on services to the organization, and the EAP's role as the employer's expert consultant on human dynamics in the workplace has often diminished. This has occurred for a number of reasons. First, as responsibility for EAPs has been delegated to benefits departments rather than employee relations or human resources offices, EAPs have been defined more narrowly. Second, downward price pressures experienced by external EAPs and budget limitations imposed on internal EAPs have forced both to concentrate on the immediate needs of individuals at the expense of larger organizational issues. Finally, some EAPs have chosen to define themselves as primarily clinical and individually focused rather than as independent problem-solvers serving both individuals and the employer" (21). Blair also cites a study of human resources managers sponsored by EAPA in 1996, which indicated "that most human resources managers understood what EAPs are, valued them, considered them inexpensive, and had no intention of canceling them. But they did not see EAPs as highly visible programs, nor did they have high expectations for them. In short, they saw an EAP as 'nice to have' but not a contributor to the organization" (21–22). Everything that Blair is stating here is entirely accurate and is confirmed by my own experience with employee assistance programs and employers. But the question is: Why is there so much misunderstanding among employers and, indeed, among employee assistance practitioners, as to what employee assistance is and is not? Blair herself raises the same question "How is it possible that a profession with standards, definitions, and a Core Technology can seem so ill-defined and amorphous to its customers?" (21).

The remainder of Blair's article describes several things that employee assistance programs can do to provide "full value" to employers, among them, "[c]onsultation," becoming "proactive and consultative," and defining "consultation as valuable in and of itself" (22–23). Although all of Blair's suggestions would, if implemented, contribute greatly to employer understanding of employee assistance and more effective EAPs, they ultimately miss the point—they are effects rather than causes—for the confusion experienced by employers has its source in the confusion in the profession itself as to what constitutes an employee assistance program and what does not. To cite just one instance: The profession's endorsement of managed mental health care literally guarantees that EAPs will devote most of their efforts to clinical activities. Once the major emphasis becomes that of realizing the imperatives of the managed mental health care industry, the EAP practitioner's focus is diverted from the worksite and its dynamics to that of functioning as a gatekeeper for the managed mental health care program. How could it be otherwise? Here again, we are confronted with the problem of integrated health care delivery systems and their purposes. Until we admit that there is an enormous amount of confusion and, indeed, obfuscation, in the profession itself, and address it, it is useless to lament the confusion among employers. We will examine this issue in greater detail in Part III.

Another article in the same issue of the *Exchange* is by John "Mickey" McKay and is entitled "Time to Reclaim Our Profession." In keeping with the theme under consideration, McKay, who is described "as labor director on the EAPA Board of Directors," writes the following: "The answer to 'What is an EAP?' is that it is constantly evolving, and we must be willing to adapt to these changes if we are going to be successful" (29). This is an extraordinary statement. I can only imagine what might be in the mind of a prospective corporate client who, upon inquiring as to the nature and purpose of employee assistance, is told that "it"—whatever "it" is—is "constantly evolving." McKay's response to the question not only ignores EAPA's definition of employee assistance but presents us once more with that magical concept of change, which is used to brush aside definitions, principles, and standards. Moreover, the title of his essay, "Time to Reclaim Our Profession," is misleading;

there is nothing in the body of the text that speaks to the idea of reclaiming "Our Profession." If Blair wants to know why there is confusion among employers about employee assistance, she need look no further than the words of some of her colleagues in the profession. McKay's response to the question "What is an EAP?" is almost a guarantee that human resource managers and others will continue to look upon employee assistance programs as "nice to have" but as contributing little or nothing to organizational development.

Still another article in this issue is entitled *"Do We Need a Commonly Accepted Definition?"* The author, Helene King, who is described as "the external providers director on the EAPA Board of Directors," states the following: "So, what is an EAP? Does our field even need a commonly accepted definition?" Immediately following these two questions are the following statements: "I believe we have the job of educating our customers and their brokers about the EAP Core Technology. But from a business perspective, the EAP will evolve as the businesses of our customers evolve" (29–30). Again, we have a refusal to address some of the most pressing issues in the profession today. First, King is not sure that we "even need a commonly accepted definition" of employee assistance and, second, evinces ambivalence about the relationship of the Core Technology to employee assistance and to corporate clients because both will, after all, "evolve."

If this brief review of some of the contents of recent issues of the *Exchange* demonstrate anything at all, it is that many members of the profession, including its leadership, have lost sight of the nature, structure, and purpose of employee assistance. As the result of either ignorance or willful obfuscation, some employee assistance practitioners take a kind of laissez-faire attitude—employee assistance can be anything we wish to make it; some put their faith in what they believe to be the transformative qualities of change, whatever that may mean; some believe it is no longer capable of standing by itself, or, indeed, that it should, but must become part of more comprehensive integrated health care delivery systems. We could continue the litany, but I think enough has been said to demonstrate that the current state of employee assistance is one of dissolution. We will look at the roots of the problem in Chapter 2.

Chapter 2

THE ROOTS OF THE PROBLEM

The problem, simply put, is that the profession generally and its leadership in particular have, for a variety of reasons, lost sight of the nature and purpose of employee assistance. Like a balloon that has lost its moorings, the profession is at the mercy of constantly shifting winds. Or, to vary the metaphor somewhat, it is like a ship at sea without a compass, drifting aimlessly and with no destination in sight. As Paul Roman observed in the February 1996 issue of *Employee Assistance*, the field is adrift. "In a very significant way, EA work as a field of activity is not marching[,] but[,] rather, drifting towards its destiny. As I have repeatedly observed, the EA field has suffered under leadership that refuses to define boundaries. Prominent leaders seem to refuse to see the huge value associated with 'laying distinctive claim' on the field's core technology (however that may be defined). Instead, there is this vision of opportunity-seeking . . . the mentality seems to be 'let's see what's on the next bandwagon of fads, and it's all right to board that one too'" (21).

In my judgment, Roman is correct. In many respects the field has changed dramatically since I first entered it. I attended my first AL-MACA (now EAPA) conference in October 1979 in Detroit, Michigan, and being relatively new to the profession at that time was very fortunate in that the presentations at the conference were on the essential conceptual framework of employee assistance: supervisor training, the role of the supervisor in an EAP, and, generally, the philosophy and mechanics of employee assistance. I believed then, and still believe today, that I came away from that conference with a sound introduction to the essential nature and purpose of employee assistance. Put another way: I was introduced to the *principles* of employee assistance.

Almost 10 years later, in May 1989, I attended a regional EAPA conference in Tulsa, Oklahoma, and was surprised, to put it mildly, by the extraordinary differences in substance and tone between this conference and the one in Detroit in 1979; not one of the presentations at the Tulsa conference was addressed to traditional employee assistance concepts. Rather, we heard presentations on topics such as cocaine-only treatment programs, managed care, and employee assistance as primarily a counseling activity. I was initially trained as a historian, and the thought that came to me then, as it has since then, is that when institutions lose sight of their origins ("certain particular treasures of the past"), that is, when they sever themselves from the roots that give them life and sustenance, they eventually wither and die or at best become pale imitations of what they were designed to be.

If anything, the tendency to nullification of traditional employee assistance practice and principles has intensified in recent years. Much of the professional literature in the field focuses on topics such as drug testing programs, clinical activities, managed mental health care, and treatment programs of one kind or another. Indeed, a layperson, hoping to learn something about employee assistance from the literature, might be inclined to believe, after reviewing the literature, that employee assistance is drug testing, clinical activities, managed mental health care, and treatment. With the exception of Paul Roman's work and that of a few others, one reads very little these days about the essential nature and purpose of employee assistance; traditional employee assistance concepts such as supervisor training, constructive confrontation, and early identification of the troubled employee on the basis of impaired job performance are infrequently referenced. It seems as if the worksite—both conceptually and practically—has disappeared from the vocabulary of the profession. To cite just a few instances: Of more than thirty essays in one volume on employee assistance, just a few make reference to supervisor training and then only briefly. One essay (Farmer and Maynard, 35) in fact suggests that "[i]f no regular supervisory or management training occurs in the company, it may not be appropriate to conduct formal EAP training either." This is almost like saying that an illiterate person, because she is illiterate, should not be taught to read and write. Another essay (Manuso) in the same volume addresses the role of the Occupational Clinical Psychologist (OCP) in business and industry and emphasizes the functions of the OCP as educator, clinician, tester, and corporate manager and employee. The following passages are representative of the tone and substance of the essay:

> Because a small proportion of employees accounts for the majority of problem behaviors, personality tests may effectively predict and select out those individuals. (158)

> The educator role is critically important for contemporary OCP, for the practitioner must train, educate, and teach the managerial class in the behavioral methods of self-improvement, and in the management of employees and organizations, both large and small. The occupational clinical psychologist, as change agent, is an educator turned consultant. (159)

> The employee must be socialized in the ways of the corporation—the corporate code must be adhered to, the corporation's myths publicly accepted, and its members and hierarchy learned. (160)

Apart from the breathtaking arrogance of these statements, their dubious assertions bordering on psychobabble, and the stilted and pompous language that is almost totalitarian in nature, one wonders what any of this has to do with employee assistance. Moreover, one is left with the impression that employee assistance programs—if indeed employee assistance is what Manuso is talking about—are designed to be big brothers, gurus, and cheerleaders. Much of what the essay suggests—especially the emphasis on personality testing—has no place in an EAP and no place in a corporation. And nothing in the essay indicates any awareness of the nature and purpose of employee assistance—this in a volume the subtitle of which is *Principles and Practice of Employee Assistance Programs.*

But the lack of understanding of employee assistance—willful or otherwise—is not confined solely to professional journals and books. In personal conversations with people working in the employee assistance field, both here in Wichita and elsewhere in the country, I am constantly struck by the confusion and obfuscation present in the field today. At local EAPA chapter meetings, guest speakers talk about everything under the sun—HMOs, inpatient treatment, outpatient treatment, vocational training, family therapy, and social work, to name just a few of the topics—everything, that is, except employee assistance. In the past five years, for example, I have not heard one speaker address the topic of supervisor training or constructive confrontation.

But the question remains: Why has employee assistance abandoned its principles and practice and adopted a policy of expediency? Why has it, in other words, abandoned the worksite—the only context in which it has any meaning and the only context in which it can have any meaning—to become no more than an appendage of whatever fad or trendy notion appears on the horizon. Even to begin to answer those questions requires that we start with the broadest possible perspective, for one reason if for no other: Employee assistance does not exist in isolation. Like every other institution in society, it acts upon and is acted upon by a variety of social, economic, political, and cultural forces, all of which are vying with one another for, if not supremacy, at least a forum where their voices may be heard.

In a very real sense, then, the problem is much larger than employee assistance. It is broadly cultural and involves many if not most of the institutions in our society; in education, in the arts, in government at all levels, in business, in journalism, and in literature generally, there have been fundamental changes in how these institutions function and in how they relate to one another. Perhaps the most fundamental change of all is the deliberate effort to soften or do away with standards, that is, principles and norms. And the rationale most often cited for doing so is that standards are too restrictive and inhibit "creativity," whatever that may mean. That standards are restrictive is correct; indeed, they are meant to be restrictive, for such restriction creates the very basis for the possibility of knowledge. Whether standards are the result of custom, convention, or authority, they are designed to focus our minds on the nature and purpose of an object and to provide guidelines as to what is and what is not intrinsic and essential to that object. Only thus do we acquire knowledge.

Standards are also annoying. At some point and at some clearly defined level standards compel us to evaluate our thinking and our behavior and, implicitly at least, bring us up short when we deviate from or violate those standards. Standards are how we judge the veracity of ideas and behaviors and come to at least tentative conclusions about the world and ourselves. Standards, in other words, invite, indeed compel, us to say no when it is necessary to do so. Absent standards we are left with an intellectual and moral void or what philosophers and theologians call nihilism, an absence of meaning and purpose. For the nihilist, there is no objective ground of truth, intellectually or morally. To abolish standards, then, is to create an environment wherein objects are indistinguishable from one another, thus setting the stage for confusion and intellectual and moral paralysis. In short, truth is the casualty.

Thus, however much we may disdain concepts such as truth, even truth with a small "t", and however much we may abhor words such as standard, principle, norm, or authority, we cannot dispense with them, for one reason if for no other: They provide us with guidelines that are both necessary and prudential. And this is the concern that animates much of the work of Paul Roman; writing in the July 1990 issue of *Employee Assistance* (p. 9), he addresses what is perhaps the single most important issue in the field of employee assistance today, namely, the issue of *principles* and their importance in delineating and maintaining the nature of an object, in this case, employee assistance. He puts it this way: "The *basic issue* is whether EA work is centered on an agreed-upon set of principles and techniques or whether EA work is a loose confederation of individuals marketing whatever 'human services' decision-makers in the workplace may find attractive" (italics added). Those in the field of employee assistance cannot, Roman rightly maintains, have it both ways; they cannot espouse an integral set of principles that define the nature and purpose of employee assistance and at the same time discard those principles in an effort to be trendy, up-to-date, or merely expedient. The two positions are mutually exclusive. Principles, then, like standards, are evaluative; they subject behavior to criteria in order to determine that which is essential to an object as that object and that which is not. Principles permit us to say no.

The New Shorter Oxford English Dictionary (hereinafter the *OED*) defines the word principle in several ways, among them, "A fundamental truth or proposition on which others depend . . . a primary assumption [an axiom] forming the basis of a chain of reasoning" and "A fundamental quality or attribute determining the nature of something, (an) essence." What all of these definitions have in common is the idea of both intrinsicality and exclusion, the latter by virtue of the former. A thing is what it is by virtue of what is intrinsic or essential to its nature, and without which it would not be what it is. But to say that something is what it is by virtue of its essential nature is also to suggest that it is exclusionary, that is, it excludes elements foreign to its nature, which, if included, would change the nature of the object. Principles, in other words, are fundamental or axiomatic; they determine within narrow boundaries the activities and tendencies of an object and serve to distinguish between that object and other objects. Thus, principles are also restrictive, and this is the point of Roman's statement when he says that "[c]entering the field on an agreed-upon set of principles and ideas implies rigidity and a lack of adaptability to changing demands." Moreover, "it would appear there are heavy prices to pay for the EA field being grounded in a set of agreed-upon principles. Indeed, such a grounding implies *there are activities in the workplace which EA workers cannot and should not do"* (italics added). Either employee assistance is centered "on an agreed-upon set of principles and ideas" or it is not; it cannot be centered on a clearly delineated and fundamental set of principles and at the same time not be centered on those principles. It will be one or the other, but not both. In view of the intellectual and moral confusion (recall Sharar and White's words about the ethical discord in the behavioral health care industry) that permeates our society today, Roman's words remind us that principles are not archaic but fundamental and, therefore, necessary.

Indeed, Roman's words go right to the heart of the issue, for if employee assistance professionals are serious about maintaining the integrity of the field, then they, and they alone, not employers or corporations, and certainly not whimsy, fashion, or the lure of lucrative managed mental health care contracts, should determine what employee assistance is and what it is not and what it should do and what it should not do. As Roman puts it: "[A] commitment to principles means that EA workers, rather than workplace consumers, will have 'the last word' in determining the design and nature of what will become delivered under the rubric of EA services." If the employee assistance field is to maintain its integrity, it cannot be otherwise.

Roman is also right on another issue, namely, that of paying a heavy price for adherence to principles. Since principles are the major obstacle to expediency or fashion, it is almost certain, at least in the short run, that the individual or institution, which insists on the primacy of principles, will experience a decline in status, popularity, and even income. But the reverse is also true; in the long run principles will be triumphant, for one reason if for no other: They more accurately describe the nature of reality and in so doing point us in the direction of that which is essential and therefore compelling. The choice for employee assistance professionals, then, is this: Abandon principles for short-term gain and almost certain long-term dissolution, or maintain the integrity of the field by adhering steadfastly to principles and prosper in the long run. This is the proverbial "fork in the road."

The presence or absence of principles, Roman suggests, is the difference between the professional and the entrepreneur. For the professional, principles, no matter how restrictive, will determine the nature and purpose of her activities; for the entrepreneur, on the other hand, principles are merely obstacles to expediency. It would be well if Roman's words were taken to heart by employee assistance practitioners.

In the same issue of *Employee Assistance* (July 1990), Bradley Googins makes essentially the same point: "While the ultimate EAP activities should reflect a constant interaction between the EAP mission and corporate needs, the EAP has the responsibility of actively, even aggressively, promoting the 'family' values and boundaries of who we are and what we stand for. . . . We need to do a better job letting our corporations and the corporate world know what we stand for and how our mission can be useful to the broader corporate mission and goals" (29).

If these words were applicable twelve years ago, they are even more so today, for employee assistance, at least as we have traditionally understood it, is presently confronted by a troubling but not altogether unusual paradox: At a time when it has achieved a certain public recognition, it is on the verge of self-destructing. If we measure success in terms of recognition or visibility, there is no question that employee assistance is successful, but if we measure it substantively, that is, in terms of its traditionally stated purposes and goals, the story is quite different. Running the gamut from those who would like to jettison the entire traditional structure of employee assistance, including the core technology, in favor of whatever employers would like it to be, to those who would like to create super EAPs, to those who would like to "integrate" employee assistance and managed mental health care, to those who would like to emphasize therapy at the expense of assessment and referral, there are movements afoot designed to make employee assistance something it cannot be without abandoning every one of its principles and changing the field beyond recognition. Fascinated by innovation and driven by a certain hubris, there are those in the field who would like to abandon principles and strike out in new directions.

That precisely this kind of confusion and obfuscation reign supreme in the employee assistance field was pointed out by Paul Roman in the January 1994 issue of *Employee Assistance*. Writing about what he sees as the "growing turmoil" in the field, Roman states that "[i]ncreasingly fierce competition is found within the EA field itself and between EA workers and those in emergent peripheral areas such as managed care and behavioral health. Entrepreneurialism seems to have achieved dominance over professionalism" (17). Again, Roman is correct. And he is not alone in his concerns about the direction employee assistance is taking. In his excellent book, *Behavioral Risk Management,* Rudy Yandrick makes much the same point. Speaking of those EAPs "which view themselves as extensions of the healthcare delivery system rather than workplace resources to reduce behavioral risks," he suggests that "their philosophy is reflected in the fact that they are sometimes sold by healthcare organizations to employers as a free add-on service when the employer is already a customer for healthcare services" (342). The problem, Yandrick maintains, is that "in the behavioral risk management paradigm, the EAP is primarily a workplace problem assessment resource whose mission is to identify and diminish behavioral risks, not to be a long-term therapeutic tool for resolving behavioral health problems" (343). Yandrick's words go right to the heart of the matter, for to describe employee assistance as "primarily a workplace problem assessment resource whose mission is to identify and diminish behavioral risks" is to describe it accurately and precisely. It is the worksite, not the therapist's office, that should be the primary focus of employee assistance.

As we have already seen, confusion and obfuscation are the only words that can be used to describe accurately the kind of thinking taking place in the employee assistance field today. Caught up in a kind of love-hate relationship with managed mental health care, on the one side, and mesmerized by a black hole of standardless activity, on the other, many EAPs have become opportunistic, desperately trying to patch together some kind of justification that they hope will provide them with a semblance of legitimacy. Sturdivant's "strategic alliances" are just one such example of that confusion.

Thus the absence of standards (or principles) has another debilitating effect: Faced with a complete lack of legitimacy as the result of severing themselves from their roots in the worksite, many EAPs are scurrying to find something—anything—that will provide them with a reason for being and secure their existence. Managed mental health care, which is essentially incompatible with employee assistance, is only one of the siren calls being heeded by many in the profession. Another is some variation on what I referred to above as the "black hole" approach to employee assistance, an approach that not only abandons standards but seeks to reconstitute the field by elevating a kind of nihilism to a central principle. Next to the proponents of managed mental health care, the nihilists exercise the greatest influence on the profession today. Indeed, it is probably accurate to say that the nihilists, to a very considerable degree, paved the way for the takeover of the employee assistance field by the managed mental health care industry. For that reason we will review some of their efforts in Chapter 3 and reserve our comments on managed mental health care for Part III.

Chapter 3

THE NIHILISTS AMONGST US

Nihilism can be defined as the doctrine that denies there is any objective ground of truth, even truth with a small "t"; a corollary of the doctrine of nihilism is the doctrine of relativism, the belief that there are no universal or objective ethical standards and that everything—a culture, an idea, a philosophy, and so on—is entirely relative to time, place, and circumstance. Judgments and evaluations that suggest anything to the contrary are, therefore, viewed with skepticism if not condemnation. As I suggested in Chapter 2, there is a strong strain of nihilism and its twin relativism in employee assistance today.

One example of the nihilist approach to employee assistance is to be found in an article by Elena Brown Carr (who is one of EAPA's regional directors) and Bernie McCann entitled "Reshaping EA Delivery: Small Business Challenge Tests Profession" in the March 1994 issue of *Employee Assistance*. Far from being unique, the article is representative of a growing trend in employee assistance—a trend that seeks to retain the name and form of employee assistance while at the same time emptying it of all substance. Carr and McCann attempt to address what they perceive as the needs of small business by suggesting, as their central thesis, that "EA providers must design a segment-specific product to meet this group's needs" (1). Elaborating on their thesis, they state the following: "Our sense is that small employers are suspicious of 'programs.' Some of these employers are very specific and astute about what services they desire (and are willing to pay for). Do we assume they know what is best for their businesses, or [*sic*] to use a missionary and pagans [*sic*] analogy, do we insist on bringing them into our fold, and converting them to our way of thinking before we respond to the needs they have identified" (13).

One hardly knows where to begin to understand what Carr and McCann mean when they talk about employee assistance—if employee assistance is what they are talking about—nor is there any hint anywhere in their article of just what "specific services" small employers have identified and desire. And to make matters even more opaque, the authors do not tell us how they arrived—other than to say that it is their "sense"—at the knowledge "that small employers are suspicious of 'programs'" and "are very specific and astute about what services they desire." Apart from the vagueness of these statements, the most that can be said for them is that they are merely a variation on the old nostrum that "the customer is always right," a proposition that, as suggested earlier, is at the very least dubious. Implicitly, and on another level, the very lack of anything substantive in the Carr-McCann thesis raises questions about the nature and purpose of employee assistance. Indeed, the whole point of the article seems to be that of making a distinction between "employee assistance programs" and something called "employee assistance," meanwhile suggesting that the latter has a kind of legitimacy if that is what small businesses desire. But no matter how closely one scrutinizes the article it is impossible to grasp, even remotely, what employee assistance is, at least as Carr and McCann understand it. One is left with the impression that employee assistance can be everything or nothing. Put another way: There is neither an inner core nor outer boundaries to their version of employee assistance; it appears to be no more than an amorphous mass of "services" without an anchor or a referent. That this is in fact the case is suggested by the following question in their article: "Is the priority to connect with these businesses and deliver some type of employee assistance or to strictly adhere to the core technology and offer the full broadbrush EA services only through familiar delivery mechanisms?" (18). The question, obviously, is rhetorical, and the answer, obviously, is "some type of employee assistance."

Having consigned the Core Technology to oblivion, Carr and McCann then provide us with a glimpse of what they would like to see employee assistance become: "With the potential onset of national health insurance, EA providers can ill afford to ignore the need to secure a niche in the healthcare delivery system. EA professionals need to position the profession squarely in the middle of the healthcare debate. Health planners are looking at creating statewide purchasing and delivery mechanisms paid for by employers, and it is an opportunity to become part of the healthcare service continuum" (18). The first thing to be noticed about these statements is that they bear no relationship, logical or necessary, to the notion, previously expressed, that employee assistance should offer small employers whatever services, completely unspecified, they might desire. There is an enormous conceptual and logical gap between the two propositions—that of offering small employers "some type of employee assistance" and securing "a niche in the healthcare delivery system"— and there appears, furthermore, to be no recognition of this on the part of Carr and McCann. If there is any coherence to their thesis, it can only lie in an effort to clear away the "familiar delivery mechanisms" of employee assistance in order "to become part of the healthcare service continuum." Moreover, it would be interesting to know if Carr and McCann surveyed small employers to determine if the latter would be interested in a national health insurance scheme, especially since, as they acknowledge, it would be those small employers who would have to pay for it.

Like much of the rest of the essay, the statements cited above not only discard the traditional tenets of employee assistance principles and practice but leave us wondering what employee assistance might become in the minds of some of its practitioners. At no point in these statements, for example, is there any indication as to how employee assistance would "become part of the healthcare delivery continuum" or, more importantly, why it should.

Second, to suggest that EAPs become part of a health care delivery system is not only to minimize the importance of the principles and practice of employee assistance but to underscore Paul Roman's point that the entrepreneur has subjugated the professional in the employee assistance field. Thus the dilemma posed by the Carr-McCann version of employee assistance is not only a conceptual one but a practical one as well, involving, as it does, how EAPs present themselves to employers, how they specify the kinds of services they offer, and, last but not least, how they respond to the employee who needs their help. Another way of saying this is that employee assistance as a profession, like all professions, *must include both a well-defined and principled conceptual framework and clear guidelines for practice.* Implicitly or explicitly, practice and principle are dependent on one another; practice that is not guided by principles becomes aimless and erratic, and principles that are not anchored in practice are likely to become no more than empty abstractions. Other than to suggest that we offer small employers "some type of employee assistance" and that employee assistance practitioners "become part of a healthcare delivery system," Carr and McCann offer nothing in the way of a principled framework for understanding employee assistance and consequently nothing in the way of clear guidelines for employee assistance practice.

Finally, the Carr-McCann thesis is, obviously, inconsistent; we are told, on the one hand, that EAPs should offer some type of employee assistance and, on the other, that EAPs need to secure a niche in the health care delivery system. Perhaps the inconsistency is more apparent than real since the Carr-McCann version of employee assistance is devoid of anything substantive, and healthcare delivery can just as easily be labeled employee assistance as anything else. The problem, however, is that employee assistance is not, as Roman, Yandrick, and others have pointed out, and as we shall see in subsequent chapters, health care delivery. This brings us full circle to the problem at the heart of the Carr-McCann thesis—the problem of unprincipled or standardless activity in all nihilist versions of employee assistance.

The issues raised in the Carr-McCann essay represent merely the tip of the iceberg and do not exhaust the almost limitless variety of nihilist versions of employee assistance. One has only to recall the McKay and King essays in the March/April 2002 issue of the *Exchange* to acknowledge the veracity of that statement. Nor do the issues raised in the Carr-McCann essay tell us why the employee assistance field is in the predicament it is or why so many of its practitioners have discarded all standards. If the flaws in the Carr-McCann version of employee assistance are obvious, the underlying causes are less so; they are sometimes subtle, sometimes masked by good intentions, and sometimes merely the result of a lack of knowledge or training.

Obviously, the question is why. Why has employee assistance, in some cases at least, moved so far away from its traditional conceptual framework and practice to embrace—sometimes eagerly—concepts and practice that are not only peripheral but even inimical to its principles? Why do some employee assistance practitioners believe they can sever employee assistance from its roots in the worksite and still have something called "employee assistance"? There are, I believe, several reasons.

First, either through ignorance, purposeful forgetting, or expedience, some of those who work in the field view it as not quite substantial, as not having well-defined principles and practice, and therefore as not quite legitimate. Their stance is essentially apologetic. Unwilling or unable to set firm boundaries or enunciate clear and concise principles, they dispense with all boundaries and all principles and, in a manner of speaking, invite all and sundry to partake of the form, if not the substance, of employee assistance. What else would explain the unseemly haste with which some EAPs have embraced programs such as drug testing and managed mental health care, to name just two of the better known attractions? It is almost as if they are casting about wildly to appropriate something of substance, the absence of which might cast doubt on the legitimacy of their programs. No doubt part of the problem is that unlike other areas or disciplines within the human services field, employee assistance deals with an extraordinarily wide variety of issues and problems that are not only directly related to the worksite but sometimes call for the skills of a diplomat and are not always easily amenable to tidy solutions. The employee assistance consultant has to be able to relate to and work with a wide variety of people and personalities in situations that are frequently fluid, unpredictable, and not amenable to quick or facile solutions. In many cases, the consultant, in order to resolve particular issues or problems with particular employees or employers, may be working with supervisors, labor representatives (if the company is unionized), and other employees, all in an effort to resolve a seemingly intractable problem. And given the inexhaustible variety of problems and personalities in such situations, the potential for conflict or misunderstanding is great and the potential for satisfactory solutions not easily discernable; it may be just this kind of uncertainty that creates doubt about the legitimacy or orthodoxy of employee assistance in the minds of some practitioners. All of this is but another way of saying that for some EAP practitioners, the frequent absence of certainty, or at least boundaries or mechanisms for ensuring a degree of control over the wide variety of problems and issues that can emanate from the worksite, calls into question the very legitimacy of employee assistance. Unlike other areas in the human services field—such as social work and clinical psychology where, theoretically at least and notwithstanding the fact that the results have not come close to approximating the promise, there is a body of doctrine that claims to be able to account for all problems and eventualities—the destination for the employee assistance practitioner may be remote, the terrain rocky, and the outcome uncertain. Again, however, in many instances, the problem can be traced to a willful disregard of, and even contempt for, the principles and practice of employee assistance. In any case, the lack of conceptual understanding and practice creates uncertainty and confusion.

Lacking the stability afforded by traditional employee assistance principles and practice and consigned, as a result, to existing on the margins of the company, these EAPs become easy targets for whatever nostrums appear on the horizon. They are in essence empty, thus very vulnerable to whatever fad or trend purports to assist employers and employees. Haunted by the feeling that they lack substance and integrity, their tendency is to look outside themselves to find something that will provide them with a sense of identity. This is not very different from those persons who perceive themselves as lacking an identity and who are forever trying to "find" themselves. As Eric Hoffer and others have pointed out, these are the people who provide the fodder for mass movement ideologies (the codependency movement is a good example) and who gravitate from one movement to another—frequently contradictory movements—not because they understand or believe in the movement but merely because the movement, temporarily at least, offers some respite from their emptiness. For the time being, they can experience something akin to an identity.

Second, and this too is a result of the absence of principles, many EAPs have emphasized means to the exclusion of ends. Perhaps another way of saying this is that in the absence of principles, standards, or norms, there is the very real danger that technique and the application of technique become ends in themselves. And the exclusion of ends, no matter how formidable the techniques, leaves the means vulnerable to questionable applications. When standards, principles, or norms are absent, there is no guiding principle, no prescription of any kind, and no boundaries; there is, in short, no way to know what is and what is not determinative of a particular endeavor or idea. It is the absence of normative guidelines that explains the entrepreneur Paul Roman has written about and that is so vividly demonstrated in the Carr-McCann version of employee assistance. We will see that same absence of principles, standards, or norms when we discuss managed mental health care and efforts to integrate it and employee assistance.

Third, and this is a relatively new development, recent years have seen an extraordinary increase in the number of mental health professionals working in employee assistance programs. People with master's and doctoral degrees in several different but related disciplines—such as clinical psychology, social work, and marriage and family therapy, among others—are finding employment in the field. Indeed, some professional organizations in the human services field are actively encouraging their members to seek employment in the employee assistance field; employee assistance programs, they are told, provide opportunities to practice therapy. On balance, the results have been mixed. On the positive side, most mental health professionals working in employee assistance programs possess sophisticated clinical skills and a broad knowledge of community resources. They also bring to their clinical activities dedication of a very high order.

Ironically, however, it is these very same skills, training, and knowledge that prevent many mental health professionals from understanding the nature and purpose of employee assistance. Because they have been trained as clinicians, the clinical perspective, with its emphasis on therapy, almost by definition rules out any idea not directly related to the clinical. Put another way: The clinical perspective is an all-encompassing one, including as it does not only a knowledge of pathology, but also, implicitly at least, some conception of the nature of human nature and an almost unqualified belief in the efficacy of therapy. Thus the clinical approach is much broader than its merely remedial function would suggest; contrary to what empiricists in clinical fields might believe or suggest, every school of psychology contains a metaphysics. Philip Rieff makes this point brilliantly in his book, *The Triumph of the Therapeutic: Uses of Faith after Freud.* In the closing paragraph of the book, Rieff, speaking of the "therapeutics," that is, the purveyors of therapeutic doctrine, has this to say: "The therapeutics must be understood precisely in their efforts to go beyond the analytic attitude, as the articulate representatives of a sharp and probably irreparable break in the continuity of Western culture. None of their doctrines promises an authentic therapy of commitment to communal purpose; rather, *in each the commitment is to the therapeutic effort itself. . . . The therapy of all therapies is not to attach oneself exclusively to any particular therapy, so that no illusion may survive of some end beyond an intensely private sense of well-being to be generated in the living of life itself. That a sense of well-being has become the end, rather than a by-product of striving after some superior communal end, announces a fundamental change of focus in the entire cast of our culture*" (261, italics added).

These are powerful and, some would suggest, controversial words, but anyone who has any knowledge of or training in psychology knows them to be accurate. What Rieff is suggesting here is that the "therapeutics"— and more broadly, psychology—have made a determined and largely successful effort to supplant the cosmologies, religious and secular, which have shaped the course of Western culture for at least two millennia. For the therapeutics, salvation is to be found *"in the therapeutic effort itself,"* not in therapy as such, for the therapeutic effort is much more than therapy. It does not propose merely to address a particular emotional or psychological problem but to announce a way of life; it is, in short, a kind of ideology that purports to offer the individual not only a particular way of life but also and as a result "an intensely private sense of well-being." It suggests a philosophy of life—actually, a faith—rather than merely a remedy for problems.

"[I]n each the commitment is to the therapeutic effort itself," and "no illusion may survive of some end beyond an intensely private sense of well-being," are words that should be read and pondered over and over again. For Rieff's point here is essential to understanding the impact of the therapeutics on our culture generally and on institutions particularly, including employee assistance. If I understand him correctly, what Rieff is explicating here is an extreme form of nominalism, the idea that universals or abstract concepts—such as society and community—are mere names without any corresponding reality. The nominalist sees only specific individuals or specific concrete entities as having any basis in reality, thus he denies the existence or the reality of anything beyond individuals and entities. And the therapeutic—essentially a nominalist—sees the individual as the only substantive carrier of norms, values, and beliefs and his well-being as the only legitimate end of the therapeutic effort. Communal ends, if they are considered at all, are very secondary and considered relatively unimportant to the stability and well-being of the individual. The net effect is to detach the individual from the surrounding culture, that is, communal ends, and make him the sole repository of the true and the good, however these may be defined by the individual. Thus the person is isolated, that is, he becomes a religion of one, and communal ends are attenuated. The implication in such a turn of events has consequences for employee assistance, for there is a corresponding pattern between the "intensely private sense of well-being" advocated by the therapeutics and the retreat of employee assistance from the worksite. In focusing exclusively on the individual employee-client, employee assistance abandons the worksite, and the community that is the worksite, thus isolating the person from the support available in that community. But there is more to it. In ministering only to the individual, those employee assistance programs that have abandoned the worksite set in motion a process that is circular in nature: By isolating the individual from the community that is the worksite, communal ends are attenuated, thereby isolating the individual even more and further draining the community of whatever support might have been available in the latter.

Just a brief perusal of the literature in the field of psychology indicates the extent to which American culture has been conquered by the therapeutics and the extent to which Rieff is correct when he suggests that the purpose of the therapeutics is to promote "an intensely private sense of well-being" with little regard for communal ends. One doesn't have to read a great deal to encounter words and phrases such as "boundaries," "assertiveness," "individualism," and "autonomy" or "radical autonomy," to name just a few, all of which suggest an aggressive effort to further the development of a kind of individualism that recognizes no authority beyond the self, and that, moreover, implies that happiness or a sense of well-being are to be defined by and found solely within the autonomous self.

If this were the whole of the story, that would be concern enough, but as Bernie Zilbergeld and others have suggested, present-day psychology goes far beyond enshrining radical autonomy and personal well-being as the ideals. In his *The Shrinking of America: Myths of Psychological Change*, Zilbergeld suggests that psychology is manufacturing whole new categories of mental illness: "Providing psychological services only for the sick and the seriously distressed was too limiting for many therapists. 'Therapy is too good to be limited only to the sick,' say Erving and Miriam Polster, two highly respected gestalt therapists. They continue: 'Psychotherapists who have been used to thinking of the individual, the dyad, and the small group have recently glimpsed the vast opportunities and the great social need to extend to the community at large those views which have evolved from their work with troubled people.' Those who are mentally distressed need counseling, and so do those who aren't" (91). Everyone, in short, is ripe for therapy, and, as Zilbergeld suggests, psychologists "really do intend that all of life should be included in their sphere of influence." One glance at the *Diagnostic and Statistical Manual of Mental Disorders IV (DSM IV)* should be enough to convince anyone of the truth of Zilbergeld's statements.

Whether one agrees or disagrees with Rieff and Zilbergeld, there is no question that psychology has forsaken the realm of science for the realm of ideology. The new shorter *Oxford English Dictionary (OED)* defines ideology as "a system of ideas or way of thinking . . . regarded as justifying actions and esp. to be maintained irrespective of events." It is the phrase "irrespective of events" that accounts for the distortions of reality found in all ideologies. Ideologies are self-contained systems of ideas that purport to explain all of reality and have as their essential premise the notion that human nature is infinitely plastic, therefore infinitely malleable. This is the state at which psychology has arrived; not only has it taken all of human thought and behavior for its province but it even suggests that it has all of the answers for society's problems. Citing the work of psychologist George Albee, Zilbergeld provides us with an overview of a theme that is today all too familiar in psychology particularly and the social sciences generally: "One of the most vocal advocates of prevention is psychologist George Albee. Starting with the idea that 'our social problems are all human problems, and we are the experts on those,' he urges mental health workers to become 'radical social activists proselytizing for changes in our society.' Albee and others think that psychological problems are caused by a dehumanized and unsupportive society . . . and the way to prevent problems is to change the nature of our society. Since society by definition includes all the people, groups, and institutions in the country, adoption of Albee's views would allow therapists to intrude into every single aspect of life" (92–93). This is an accurate portrait of the ideologue, one who believes that he has all of the answers for society's problems and who will not be deterred by anything contrary to his ideology or by evidence that suggests his beliefs are flawed. It is but a short step from proclaiming the omnipotence of ideology to sacrificing the legitimate interests of those whom ideologues would make the beneficiaries of their ideas. And herein lies the problem for employee assistance: There is an enormous practical and conceptual gap between the interests of clinicians and the interests of employers. Where the former see EAPs as places to practice therapy or as health care delivery systems or as opportunities for restructuring society, the latter are primarily interested in something much more mundane—behavioral risk management. Paul Roman focuses the issue clearly in the January 1994 issue of *Employee Assistance* when he states that "[m]any EA workers, along with many of their leaders, are convinced that clinical skills and activities are the centerpiece of their activities" (17). And in acting on those beliefs, they undermine that which is distinctive about employee assistance and diminish its ability to address a wide variety of worksite issues and problems. Again, Roman: "If EA workers could recognize their work is not primarily clinical, they would have a firm base upon which to build claims for how EA work adds value to a range of existing organizational functions."

Their protestations to the contrary notwithstanding, many mental health professionals do not see employee assistance as a valid or legitimate field of endeavor in and of itself, but merely another opportunity for therapy or a kind of referral service designed only to channel people into the therapist's office. Unable or unwilling to see the relationship of employee assistance to the worksite, many mental health professionals ignore the link between the troubled employee and worksite behavior problems, focus entirely on clinical activities, and, in so doing, attenuate the critical connection between employee assistance and the worksite. They place employee assistance outside of and beyond the only context that can sustain it, and in the process nullify its potential for the resolution of worksite problems.

Moreover, to see employee assistance as a health care delivery system or merely as a way of directing employees and family members into therapy or treatment programs of one kind or another, rather than as a means of managing behavioral risks in the worksite, is to dilute or even eliminate one of the most important of all employee assistance functions, that of providing counsel and advice to supervisors and other management people attempting to resolve any of a number of different kinds of problem situations in the workplace. Roman puts it this way: "The counseling and advisory functions can work only if EA services are visible and readily accessible to supervisors. Many of today's EAPs have no workplace presence because their only function is to act as a clinical funnel into treatment settings" (17–18). This last point must be stressed over and over again: To the degree that an employee assistance program is focused on clinical issues and therapy, to that degree it will minimize or ignore entirely issues and problems in the worksite. In effect, there will be no employee assistance presence in the worksite. Again, Roman: "Probably most important is the extent to which people in a particular workplace perceive that an EA worker possesses adequate workplace knowledge to be of help to them. If there is minimal presence in the workplace by EA specialists, the less likely it is that they will be viewed as credible sources of consultation."

Writing in the November/December 1995 issue of the *EAP Digest*, Barry Sugarman makes much the same point; speaking of what he describes as the two dominant EAP models, the "classical" and the "clinical," he suggests that the classical model (the traditional EAP program that emphasizes supervisor training, constructive confrontation, supervisor consultation, and case finding) has lost ground to the clinical model "due to the influx of so many EAP workers trained in the conventional clinical model" (22). The result, in Sugarman's view, is a kind of reversal of priorities or, perhaps more accurately, the elimination of all alternatives other than the clinical. Whereas the classical employee assistance program emphasizes issues related to problem situations in the workplace, that is, productivity—including but not limited to such concerns as employee morale and reducing health insurance utilization and turnover, all of primary interest to employers—the clinical view, Sugarman suggests, sees the employee as "the real client and the employer simply the one who pays the bills." Put another way: The classical view, because it is rooted in the worksite and functions within the context of the worksite, attempts to address the needs of both employers and employees, while the clinical view, because it is detached from the worksite, sees the employee as the only client. It is not too much to say that in the classical view, the worksite is the "client," while in the clinical view the employee and the practice of therapy are the only realities. As we will see in Part III, this has implications for the relationship between employee assistance and managed mental health care. It also reminds us of Rieff's words about the individual and communal ends.

There is yet another aspect of the therapy–mental health approach to employee assistance that has received little or no attention within the profession, and that is the connection between the influx of mental health professionals into the field and the decline in alcohol and drug referrals. When I first entered the field in 1979 and for a few years thereafter, referrals for alcohol and drug problems were in the range of 20 to 30 percent of all referrals into employee assistance programs, but within the past decade or so, these referrals have dropped off to barely more than 10 percent. Part of the problem may be traced to the lack of supervisor training in many employee assistance programs and part to the emphasis on drug testing. As for the latter, it is the case in many instances that employers are relying solely on drug testing rather than job performance issues to identify the alcoholics and addicts in their employ. It happens all too often that employees with long-standing job performance problems are referred to the EAP only after they have tested positive for an illegal substance. (In one instance, an employee who had been tardy 48 times, sometimes by as much as two and one-half hours, over a one and one-half year period, was referred to the EAP only after he tested positive for cocaine. And this is by no means an isolated case; since the advent of the Drug Free Workplace Act in the late 1980s this has become very common.) How much harm these employees have done to themselves and how much productivity has been lost is anyone's guess.

But the less than satisfactory results of drug testing and the lack of supervisor training notwithstanding, the situation is such that the great majority of mental health professionals have had little or no training in the area of assessing for alcohol and drug problems. Moreover, there are some mental health professionals who do not view alcoholism and drug addiction as primary illnesses but merely as the secondary effects of psychiatric problems. The result is a loss and sometimes a tragedy for both employers and employees. In an excellent essay entitled "Alcoholism as a Major Focus of EAPs," William R. Byers and John C. Quinn put the matter this way: "The crux of the problem for many helping professionals moving into EAP jobs is that their education and training [has] not prepared them to adequately recognize and assist persons with alcoholism. They have been trained to believe that the *effects* of drinking are a symptom of broader psychopathology. This view leads the helping professional on a never ending search for the underlying cause of alcoholic drinking that will somehow change the alcoholic's drinking. . . . What helping professionals are often missing in their formal education is awareness; that the pathological behavior in the alcoholic is chemically induced by the drug alcohol; that alcoholism needs to be addressed as a *primary* illness" (375–76). It is also the case, as Byers and Quinn suggest, "that many helping professionals have strong negative views of alcoholism that block their ability to appropriately treat alcoholism" (376).

Lest I be perceived as attempting to saddle mental health professionals with the entire onus for the decline in alcohol and drug referrals in employee assistance programs, I should note that the employee assistance profession generally has been complicit in de-emphasizing the role of alcohol and drugs in creating job performance problems. In fact, the profession itself and especially its leadership must assume a major part of the responsibility for the decline in alcohol and drug referrals in employee assistance programs. Compare the emphasis on alcohol in the Core Technology as this was developed by Terry Blum and Paul Roman in the March 1985 issue of *The Almacan* (18), with the comparative lack of emphasis in the Core Technology as it was presented by EAPA in its 1999 edition of the *EAPA Standards and Professional Guidelines for Employee Assistance Professionals* (v). First, Blum and Roman, in the sixth item of the Core Technology as they developed it: "*The centrality of employees' alcohol problems as the program focus with the most significant promise for producing recovery and genuine cost savings for the organization in terms of future performance and reduced benefits usage*" (italics in original). Now the present EAPA version, also item six: "Consultation to work organizations to encourage availability of and employee access to health benefits covering medical and behavioral problems, including, but not limited to, alcoholism, drug abuse, and mental and behavioral disorders." Gone is the "centrality" of alcohol problems in EAPA's version of the Core Technology; now it is merely one among several different kinds of problems, all apparently having equal weight in terms of worksite issues. To some degree perhaps this was inevitable with the advent of the "broad-brush" EAP, but the latter by itself does not explain the precipitous decline in alcohol referrals during the past decade. We would be on more solid ground if we look for an explanation of that decline in the conjunction of clinical interests and the interests of those promoting the integration of managed mental health care and employee assistance, on the one hand, and, on the other, the inability or unwillingness of the profession to maintain the absolutely essential relationship between employee assistance and the worksite.

Furthermore, it is simply the case that when alcohol problems, or alcoholism, loses its status as the central problem in employee assistance programs, it will become less significant as a source of employee work performance problems in the minds of EAP practitioners and, it is important to note, less significant in the minds of employers who contract for employee assistance services. But we'll let Blum and Roman make the case; the following is lengthy but well worth quoting: "[W]e urge attention to the fact that EAPs are singular in their provision of constructive attention to alcohol problems in the workplace. We recognize that EAPs have expanded in many directions in terms of the types of employee problems to which services are directed, but only EAPs offer promise in alcohol problem intervention. Furthermore, it is only in dealing with alcohol problems that EAPs have established a clearcut record of achievements across different workplaces and different degrees of program elaboration. . . . The EAP specialty is unique in its offering of a positive approach for the employed problem drinker, and the constituencies in the workplace that have developed throughout the nation know us primarily by our success in dealing with alcohol problems" (18).

Time has not diminished the significance or the veracity of Blum and Roman's words, for one reason if for no other: Explicit in their words is the idea that it has been alcohol problems that have been one of the principal anchors for employee assistance in the worksite, and absent that anchor the rootedness of employee assistance in the worksite becomes ever more tenuous. If one wants evidence for the truth of the assertion that the issue of alcohol problems in the workplace is no longer of primary importance in employee assistance programs, it is only necessary to review the literature in the employee assistance field over the past several years—essays addressed specifically to the problem of alcohol in the workplace are rare.

That Blum and Roman are accurate in suggesting the importance for employee assistance of focusing on alcohol problems in the workplace is borne out by Byers and Quinn, among others; drawing on a wide variety of research they state that "[a]lcoholism and alcohol misuse [is] the largest human problem at the workplace, due to the economic costs and pervasive impact on industry. Alcoholic employees have more absenteeism, more frequent accidents and illnesses, and a higher utilization of health care benefits and workers compensation than the average employee" (371).

What has been happening to employee assistance during the past decade or so is neither unique nor rare; it is what Paul Roman describes as the absence of principle—or what some social scientists call *relativization*—and it has been happening with increasing frequency in many if not most areas of American life, especially with standards and principles. To relativize anything—an object, entity, or idea—means to diminish in status or significance that object, entity, or idea *relative* to other objects, entities, or ideas within the same context or conceptual framework. The thing relativized is no longer accorded a privileged position and thus comes to be seen, implicitly or explicitly, as no longer as important as it once was or as no longer exercising the kind of influence it once did. In some cases relativization may not be harmful and may indeed be a positive good, but if the thing relativized is a principle, it will have consequences that go far beyond the changed status of the principle itself. In fact, to relativize a principle means usually to abolish it. This is the case with alcohol problems in the workplace as evidenced in the present version of the Core Technology. There is a direct and positive correlation between the relativization of alcohol problems in employee assistance programs and the decline in referrals for those problems. The result is a loss for both employees and employers. When we relativize anything, we need to be aware that doing so will have effects far beyond the thing that has been relativized. Indeed, the entire context within which the relativization takes place will be changed. Byers and Quinn sum up the situation this way: "It is possible that alcoholics at the workplace will no longer receive adequate attention, due to the lack of alcoholism expertise of the helping professionals and the reduced focus on alcoholism in the promotional and educational materials provided employees by the EAP" (370).

Paralleling and reinforcing the centrifugal tendencies detaching employee assistance from its roots in the worksite is the liberal political persuasion of many employee assistance professionals who view the free enterprise system and corporations with a great deal of loathing and are ever ready to become advocates for employees against employers. One young woman who holds a master's degree in social work and works for an employee assistance program in my part of the country told a colleague and me bluntly and unequivocally that the purpose of employee assistance is to protect employees from predatory employers. And there was no doubt in her mind that most employers are predators. (It would be interesting to know how she presents her EAP to prospective client companies. This is the "radical social activist" cited by Zilbergeld. It is also a portrait of the ideologue.) If this young woman's remarks were occasional or simply the result of ignorance, that would be one thing, but, unfortunately, they are not; over the years I've heard the same and similar kinds of remarks from long-term employees of employee assistance programs. Given the general social and intellectual ethos of our culture, sentiments like these are not as surprising as they might otherwise be. College- and university-trained professionals, especially those in the humanities and the social sciences, frequently come away from their classrooms with a particular distaste for the free enterprise system, the profit motive, and private property as manifestations of a corrupt, rapacious, and oppressive system designed only to make the rich richer and to deny "social justice" to the poor and the marginal.

None of this is to suggest that university- trained mental health professionals—social workers, clinical psychologists, and marriage and family therapists—be denied employment in the employee assistance field. It is, rather, to suggest that the profession develop a comprehensive educational program, the successful completion of which would result in certification and would be a prerequisite for entry into the field. I'm not at all optimistic, however, that we will see anything like this, at least not in the near future. Nor is any of this intended as a blanket indictment of the mental health profession—I work with several mental health professionals who are a credit to the field—but rather as a reminder that the possession of a university degree and clinical skills, in and of themselves, are neither a necessary nor a sufficient condition for understanding the nature and purpose of employee assistance.

Finally, the Employee Assistance Professionals Association (EAPA) must itself be held accountable for much of the confusion in the field today. We have already looked at the diminished role of alcohol problems in the workplace in EAPA's version of the Core Technology and the problems associated with it, but EAPA's irresponsibility is not limited to that. The association's attachment to managed mental health care and super EAPs (both of which we will review in some detail in Part III) and its dilution of the role of management in employee assistance programs have also contributed greatly to the problems in the field. For the moment we will look only at the diminished role of management in employee assistance programs. There is a close connection between it and the lack of supervisor training—and, indeed, the lack of other key components of employee assistance—in many employee assistance programs.

When I first entered the field, my mentors were careful to stress the fact—indeed, it was an axiom—that employee assistance is a worksite-based *management* program, the purpose of which is to help employees whose personal problems have contributed significantly to job deficiencies. It was clear from the definition that the program was company owned and management driven, and when we did supervisor training, we always emphasized the fact that the supervisor was the most important person in the implementation and maintenance of an EAP. It was the supervisor who held the keys to the kingdom, so to speak, and if the supervisor was not committed to the program it would not work. This basic conception of the indispensable role of the supervisor was also emphasized over and over again at the workshops and seminars my colleagues and I attended. Today, EAPA, in its 1999 edition of *EAPA Standards and Professional Guidelines for Employee Assistance Professionals*, defines employee assistance as "a worksite-based program designed to assist: (1) work organizations in addressing productivity issues, and (2) 'employee clients' in identifying and resolving personal concerns, including, but not limited to, health, marital, family, financial, alcohol, drug, legal, emotional, stress, or other personal issues that may affect job performance" (v). Other than to state that the program is "worksite-based," there is no suggestion in EAPA's definition that the program is company owned or that management plays a pivotal role in the implementation and maintenance of the program.

Nor is the issue made any clearer in item one of EAPA's version of the Core Technology (also page v of the *Standards*), which reads in part: "Consultation with, training of, and assistance to work organization leadership (managers, supervisors, and union stewards) seeking to manage the troubled employee, enhance the work environment, and improve employee job performance." One could reasonably infer from both the definition and item one of the Core Technology that an employee assistance program is implemented and maintained, in a word, owned, by the EAP consultant and that the company and management are merely passive recipients of services provided by the EAP. In effect, and for all practical purposes, the status of management in employee assistance programs, like that of the role of alcohol problems in the workplace, is diminished. Perhaps another way of saying this—and this is the essential point—is that the absence of the word *management* from the definition of employee assistance indicates a radical change in how EAPA perceives itself, the nature and purpose of employee assistance, and, most importantly, the nature of the relationship between employee assistance programs and the employers and employees they serve. For in excluding management from the structure of employee assistance, the profession destroyed the very integral nature of its relationship to the work organization, thereby creating a vacuum that not only diminished its effectiveness but paved the way for an easy takeover of the profession by the managed mental health care industry. More specifically, the disappearance of management from EAPA's scheme of things meant also the disappearance of two of the basic tenets of employee assistance, namely, (1) early identification of the troubled employee on the basis of impaired job performance, and (2) constructive confrontation. And with the disappearance of these went the disappearance of employee assistance. It could not have been otherwise, since only management is in a position to implement and make concrete these essential principles.

Words are not merely words; they are also signifiers and symbols in that they point not only to an object or idea but to a range of essential relationships inherent in and intrinsic to a definition of that particular object or idea as *that* particular object or idea. Thus the absence of management from the definition of employee assistance means the absence of management from employee assistance programs and makes tenuous the roots of employee assistance in the worksite by denying the importance of management to the maintenance of those roots. To describe or define employee assistance as merely a worksite-based program is to place it in limbo, outside of and beyond anyone's purview or control, except possibly that of the employee assistance consultant. But to do this is to suggest that ownership of the program is not the organization's but the consultant's. The absence of management from the definition of employee assistance goes a long way towards explaining why so many EAPs downplay supervisor training or, in the instance of the Carr-McCann version of employee assistance, abandon all standards. It is to the relativization of alcohol problems in the workplace and the diminished role of management in employee assistance programs today that we can attribute much of the failure of employee assistance, for when we relativize or diminish anything we deny its status or significance and consign it to a minor or peripheral role within the context of the whole, thus changing the structure and contours of the whole itself. In the case of employee assistance, this serves only to attenuate its roots in the worksite.

Before we end this chapter, it is important, I believe, to review in some detail another event—one that we have already mentioned briefly—that has had and continues to have profound significance for the effectiveness and future of employee assistance. Until the late 1980s, the professional association was called the Association of Labor-Management Administrators and Consultants on Alcoholism (ALMACA), the very title itself indicating the network of relationships that comprised the organization and indicating also the nature of those relationships. The present name, the Employee Assistance Professionals Association (EAPA) omits not only alcoholism but management and labor as well.

This last point is crucial for understanding what has happened to the profession and is closely related to other changes—notably that of the diminished status of management and alcohol problems in the worksite—in the profession itself and in its relationship to the worksite. Although the change of name for the profession may have been intended to more sharply define the profession as a profession, it had only negative effects, for there were several unfortunate and certainly unforeseen consequences.

First, the community explicit in the name ALMACA—a community made up of several groups, including labor, management, employees, employers, EAP consultants, and a constituency of employees with alcohol problems—was splintered; the profession, in effect, separated itself from the community that is the worksite, thereby depriving itself of the sustenance and vitality inherent in that network of relationships that had brought it into being. What had been a dynamic and comprehensive source of support for the troubled employee and the essential source of the profession's unique ability to respond to the needs of that employee and his employer were now greatly diminished. The supportive web of relationships, in which both the profession and the troubled employee had been enmeshed and that had provided both the stimulus for the profession's activities and its ability to respond to the needs of both employers and employees, was now a thing of the past. At this point, the only recourse for employee assistance programs was to become pale imitations of community mental health centers, and this they did. Second, and this is really a corollary of the first point, with the change in name, the profession served notice that it was no longer communal ends, that is, no longer the needs of employers and employees in context, but the needs of the individual client qua individual client that were paramount and, indeed, exclusive. From this it was but a short step to giving primacy to clinical activities. Third, with the retreat from the worksite signaled by the change in name of the profession, it was almost inevitable that there would be less emphasis on core EAP activities such as supervisor training and consultation with management. Fourth, and this was perhaps the most damaging of all the tendencies implicit in the change of name and subsequent perceptions of the profession, the profession *lost the ability to speak authoritatively* for the employee assistance community. In de-emphasizing the web of relationships that had constituted the community and that was clearly designated by the name ALMACA, the newly structured entity was no longer in a position to state categorically and authoritatively what was and what was not an employee assistance program. The most obvious proof of this assertion is the ease with which managed mental health care assumed control of the profession. Had the profession been cognizant of the fact that its very existence and effectiveness were inseparable from the worksite and had it retained the support of other elements within that community, it would have been much more difficult for the managed mental health care industry to achieve its takeover of the profession. Finally, in seeking to enhance the professional status of the profession, EAPA, like many other professional organizations, became enamored of the prerogatives and internal dynamics of the profession, often to the exclusion of the real and pressing needs of employers and employees. Indeed, it is difficult to read the literature in the field, especially in the *Exchange,* without becoming aware of the self-glorifying, almost otherworldly, quality of much of what is written. Mindless chatter about growth and change and strategic alliances do nothing to enhance the prestige and status of the profession. It merely confirms the perception that employee assistance has lost its way.

In a more general sense, there are two ideas that seem to be lost on the profession as a whole and the leadership in particular. The first of these—which some might consider shopworn, trite, or even banal, but that is nevertheless accurate—is that ideas, all ideas, have consequences. They may be slow to make themselves felt or they may be quick in coming, but come they will. When the profession decided to jettison its heritage, when it decided to change its name from ALMACA to EAPA, when it decided that alcohol problems in the workplace and management's role in the success of EAPs were of little or no import, and when it decided to pursue clinical activities, it set in motion a process that left it adrift and conceptually bankrupt. The consequences of this abandonment of principles were such that it is hardly possible now to speak of or describe employee assistance as a profession. As Paul Roman has suggested, employee assistance today is no more than "a loose confederation of individuals marketing whatever 'human services' decision-makers in the workplace may find attractive." And with its now almost complete separation from the worksite, it was inevitable that the consequence would be a profusion of trends and fads purporting to offer needed services to employees and employers.

The second of these ideas is that there is a close and essential relationship between function and authority. An institution—any institution—maintains its authority only to the degree that it is performing the function(s) it was designed to perform. Absent these functions, or if there is any attenuation in the realization of its functions, an institution will lose or greatly diminish its authority. At the risk of repetition, it is the loss of authority subsequent to the abandonment or repudiation of its functions or, what is the same thing, principles, that left employee assistance vulnerable to the siren call of managed mental health care. It has never been otherwise; institutions that do not reform themselves will have that reformation imposed on them by external agents, and that often means the demise of these institutions. We will explore these ideas in greater detail in the Conclusion.

Although the factors outlined above are the major ones serving to divorce employee assistance from the worksite, there is no question that there are many other factors playing a supporting role in the same effort. Both speculation and events suggest that any or all of a number of reasons accounts for the efforts to dissociate employee assistance from the worksite—the pervasiveness of the idea of "change" (the word itself has become a kind of mantra capable of creating all sorts of delusions), a desire to be politically correct, an egalitarian ideology that wishes to eliminate any trace of inequality, a fascination with social activism, or simply a desire to accommodate a kind of omnibus ideology that seeks to encompass all that is trendy and faddish. Whatever the reason or reasons, there is no question that the employee assistance field today is rudderless.

That the change of the association's name remains contentious is in evidence in a letter dated September 10, 2001, from EAPA to "Fellow EAPA Members" and signed by Linda Sturdivant, the association's president. We alluded briefly to this letter above, but it would be instructive to review it in a little more detail. The subject of the letter is the recent decision by the United Auto Workers to "discontinue supporting individual memberships in EAPA" (1) and what this may mean for the profession. Sturdivant states: "Over the years, many UAW and other labor members have stated that EAPA does not serve their needs. EAPA and its labor members have struggled over a long list of issues: the change in the association's name (from ALMACA to EAPA), the development and implementation of the CEAP certification program, and the promotion and support of state licensure laws, to name just three. A chasm slowly developed and grew, leaving members throughout the association feeling frustrated and thwarted." Several questions are in order. What, besides the three issues mentioned above, created the "chasm" between EAPA and the UAW? Was EAPA's marriage to managed mental health care a problem for the UAW? And why was the chasm between EAPA and the UAW permitted to develop and grow? Where was EAPA's leadership during this period of time?—"years," according to Sturdivant.

But it is the third paragraph on page 1 of the letter that is perhaps the most revealing of Sturdivant's and the leadership's thinking; it reads as follows: "Certainly the UAW has had, and continues to have, some legitimate concerns. The difficulty in resolving them lies in the fact that EAPA's mission is to represent, and serve the needs of, the *individual* employee assistance professional, not a group or groups of EA professionals." Again, a question: How or in what way are the concerns of the UAW legitimate? And another question: If the concerns of the UAW are legitimate, why were they not addressed and why are they not being addressed now?

Sturdivant, however, is precisely right when she states that the purpose of a professional association is *not* to serve the needs of groups or interests within the profession, for these can only be divisive. No profession can cater to groups or interests within its circle without creating an enormous potential for conflict and doing irreparable harm to the profession. Thus, when Sturdivant states that it is the needs of the individual practitioner that are paramount, she is voicing the essential premise of a profession as a profession. However, having said that, one can only lament the fact that she did not build on that premise to state clearly and unequivocally that the primary intent in serving the needs of the individual practitioner is to explicate the standards of the profession. Ultimately, it is this, the explication and maintenance of standards that is essential for both the profession and its practitioners. Sturdivant's letter is a step in the right direction.

But the roots of the problem in employee assistance are many and deep, which in and of themselves need not portend disaster if the profession and especially its leadership were willing to address and remedy them. But what the evidence suggests is that, thus far at least, there seems to be little inclination to do so. Sturdivant's letter could be the basis for a top-to-bottom reevaluation of the direction the profession has been taking, not only in terms of its relationship to the UAW or any other group but also to the development and implementation of standards.

Nihilism has many faces, but they all have one thing in common—a contempt for reality.

In Part II we will explore in some detail the necessary roots of employee assistance.

Part II

IN SEARCH OF ROOTS

Chapter 4

INTEGRATION: EMPLOYEE ASSISTANCE AND THE WORKSITE

If employee assistance is not merely an ill-defined assortment of services characterized only by some kind of relationship to employers and employees, not a vehicle for the delivery of health care, not managed mental health care, and not merely whatever anyone wishes to make of it, then what is it? What is its nature and purpose? How does it interact with the organization or institution it serves and that it is—or should be—an integral part of? How does it differ from other kinds of services within the broad range of the human services? In short, what makes it unique, and, when rightly understood and implemented, ideally suited to respond to a wide variety of problem situations in the workplace? Only a few short years ago these questions would not have to be asked; the great majority of people working in the employee assistance field knew—or professed to know—what employee assistance is and what it is not. This, unfortunately, is no longer the case.

The best place to begin to understand the nature and purpose of employee assistance—indeed, the only place where one can begin to understand what employee assistance is about and how it works—is in its relationship to the organization for which it provides services, specifically, the worksite—a relationship that all, I think, would agree exists, however much they might disagree about the nature and extent of that relationship. From its inception in the late 1940s until recently, employee assistance has been defined and circumscribed by its relationship to the worksite. *It had its origins in the worksite, its distinctive features framed by the worksite, and its nature and purpose defined by the worksite.* And this remains true today notwithstanding the increasing complexity and sophistication of the worksite.

Unlike other specializations or professions within the human services field, employee assistance is the only one that has the worksite for its exclusive focus; indeed, it is not too much to say that for employee assistance the worksite, ultimately, is the client. Whether the issue is productivity or employee personal concerns or the link between the two, employee assistance is designed to intervene in and alter the dynamics of the worksite. Writing in the January 1994 issue of *Employee Assistance*, Paul Roman characteristically goes directly to the heart of the issue when he states that employee assistance "is not a healthcare delivery system. Instead, *it is a mechanism for the resolution of a quite wide range of problem situations in the workplace* (17, italics added). These few words may well be the most important words in all of the literature on employee assistance. They should be read and pondered many times, for one reason if for no other: They tell us precisely, exactly, and succinctly what employee assistance is and what it is not. First, it is not a health care or behavioral health delivery system; it was not designed nor was it ever intended to be a vehicle for delivering clinical services or a kind of transfer station for the troubled employee on her way to the therapist's office. From its earliest days, its focus was the troubled employee whose personal problems were affecting her job performance, and its purpose was to help the employee return to full productivity through the processes of assessment, referral, and case management. Its purpose or end, in other words, was to alter the dynamics of the relationship between the employee and the functional requirements of the workplace. It is, then, "problem situations in the workplace" and the resolution of those problems that characterize employee assistance definitively and distinguish it from other kinds of human services activities. But as Brenda Blair reminds us, the resolution of problem situations in the workplace entails the provision of consultative services to employers. To be of maximum value to employers, "an EAP must know and anticipate the needs of the work organization. EAPs . . . need to ask themselves when they last had direct, personal interaction with the employer's key decision makers. These include not only the people directly responsible for managing the EAP, but also security and safety professionals, legal counsel, line managers, union officials, occupational health professionals, and others" (22). Thus it follows logically that if employee assistance is "a mechanism for the resolution of a quite wide range of problem situations in the workplace," which is the basic axiom or principle of employee assistance, then it cannot be a health care delivery system, nor can it be whatever one wishes to make of it. Second, to assume, as some employee assistance professionals do, that clinical activities are the end or purpose of employee assistance is, at the least, to mistake means for ends and, at worst, to perpetuate the notion that employee assistance is in essence no different from the local mental health center. This, in fact, is what many employers have come to believe about employee assistance, and it is the major reason why so many EAPs are ineffective and misunderstood by employers and employees. If, then, we wish to understand employee assistance, its nature and purpose, and its extraordinary potential for responding to the needs of employees and employers, we must start with Roman's simple but powerful definition of employee assistance as "a mechanism for the resolution of a quite wide range of problem situations in the workplace."

Before we explore these ideas any further, it might be useful to step back, digress a bit, and try to understand employee assistance within the broader concepts of economics and society. The broadest context and the best vantage point for understanding employee assistance is economics, especially that aspect of economics that we call the division of labor or, what is essentially the same thing, social cooperation. The latter is based on the simple premise that in the great majority of cases human beings working together to achieve a particular end or ends will be a great deal more productive than individuals working in isolation. And social cooperation is, in turn, based upon enlightened self-interest—the knowledge that the individual, if she wishes to further her own ends in the most satisfactory way possible, will have greater opportunities to do so if she helps her fellows to achieve their ends.

There is nothing new or radical in the notion of social cooperation; it has been around since the dawn of the human race and has been a major factor in technological advance and a constantly improving standard of living. Adam Smith simply made explicit what had been implicit in human behavior. And ultimately it is this—the division of labor or social cooperation—that is the fundamental or essential foundation of employee assistance. Thus it is an understanding of economics, not psychology, the role of the supervisor, not the therapist, and behavior within an organizational setting, not a diagnosis from the *DSM IV,* that are essential if we wish to understand employee assistance. For it is the worksite, the quintessential form of social cooperation, that is and should be the proper focus for employee assistance. The structure and dynamics of the worksite and its interdependencies and integrated activities are what give form and meaning to that which we call employee assistance. Apart from these, employee assistance has no meaning.

None of this is to suggest that the troubled employee occupies a secondary or subordinate role in the EAP scheme of things; it is, rather, to suggest that problematic employee behavior can be understood and addressed only within the context of the worksite and from the perspective of social cooperation. It is the worksite—indeed, it can only be the worksite—that defines the nature and purpose of employee assistance and dictates how it addresses problem situations in the workplace.

Contrast this with psychology, which has little or no interest in the worksite, the functional requirements of an institution, social cooperation, or communal ends. Its focus, as Rieff reminds us, is almost entirely that of individual well-being, and where it does indicate an interest in communal ends or purposes, it is increasingly for ideological rather than scientific reasons. Much of what passes for psychology today is designed to provide blueprints for utopia. Moreover, as Zilbergeld suggests, many of those who work in the field of psychology are hostile to the free enterprise system and see in it only a means of subordinating people to profits. Given its ideological nature, it's not likely that psychology will have any interest in "the resolution . . . of problem situations in the workplace," except perhaps insofar as those problem situations can be used as fodder for ideological purposes.

It is, then, economics that must be our conceptual framework for discourse about employee assistance and for addressing problem situations in the workplace. It is concepts such as the division of labor or social cooperation, productivity, and behavioral risk management—all of them essentially economic in nature—that must underlie and give form and meaning to employee assistance.

To give the preceding remarks somewhat more substance, I've drawn on the work of two of the twentieth century's greatest economists and social philosophers, Ludwig von Mises and Henry Hazlitt. In his great *Human Action: A Treatise on Economics,* von Mises suggests that human beings are rational animals who are capable of using the faculty of reason to achieve a more satisfactory state of existence: "Only the human mind that directs action and production is creative." And "[w]e call it creative because we are at a loss to trace the changes brought about by human action farther back than to the point at which we are faced with the intervention of reason directing human activities . . . [w]hat produces the product are not toil and trouble in themselves, but the fact that the toiling is guided by reason" (141–42). There is a great deal to be gleaned from these words, but for our purposes there are three essential ideas expressed here: (1) that man is possessed of the faculty of reason; (2) that through the faculty of reason he is capable of engaging and changing the world; and (3) that he is a goal-directed creature capable of intellectually formulating ends and realizing them. Man is, in other words, strongly predisposed to impose order on chaos or seeming chaos, and since he is a part of nature, it is with the materials provided by nature, that is, the mind and the world external to himself, that he directs his activities. One might object to von Mises's words on the grounds that they express no more than a commonplace or conventional view of human nature and its interaction with the natural world and as such tell us nothing new. But the importance of these words lies in the fact that they are axiomatic and constitute a kind of prologue to what von Mises calls "concerted action" or "social cooperation." It is only through cooperation with others that man relieves his uneasiness and becomes truly human. "Every step by which an individual substitutes concerted action for isolated action results in an immediate and recognizable improvement in his conditions . . . [f]or what the individual must sacrifice for the sake of society he is amply compensated by greater advantages . . . [h]e foregoes a smaller gain in order to reap a greater one" (146).

Thus, for von Mises, concerted action or social cooperation is the means by which men improve the conditions of life and create what we call society. Indeed, for von Mises, concerted action or social cooperation or, what is the same thing, the division of labor, is what makes society and all of its amenities possible. Without that concerted action or social cooperation, no society is possible. "The fundamental facts that brought about social cooperation, society, and civilization and transformed the animal man into a human being are the facts that work performed under the division of labor is more productive than isolated work and that man's reason is capable of recognizing this truth." In fact, "[in] a hypothetical world in which the division of labor would not increase productivity, there would not be any society" (144).

This last sentence may well be the most important sentence in all of von Mises's work, for what he is stating here is that without the division of labor or social cooperation, neither society nor any of those social accoutrements, which we often take for granted, would be possible. Perhaps another way of saying this is that the division of labor is not something thought up by economists or imposed arbitrarily by ruthless capitalists on helpless human beings. It arises from within the nature of things and is no more than a recognition of the nature of human nature and the nature of the physical world. Given the very ideological nature of much of our social thought—here one is reminded of Rieff's words about the therapeutics and their contempt for communal ends—it is important to emphasize that for von Mises the division of labor or social cooperation is the sine qua non for a level of human existence which permits the development of civilization and all of its amenities. Thus, *"[t]he fundamental social phenomenon is the division of labor and its counterpart human cooperation"* (157–58, italics added). The division of labor is no more than a "recognition of the laws of nature," but it is fundamental not only to providing human beings with the means of sustenance but also to the creation of that entity we call civilization, for without the social cooperation entailed in the division of labor, civilization is not possible. Moreover, "[a] pre-eminent common interest, the preservation and further intensification of social cooperation, becomes paramount and obliterates all essential collisions" (673).

Finally, for von Mises, those things that we call the division of labor or social cooperation and the human use of reason directed to the attainment of particular ends or goals all come under the heading of "conduct popularly called economic," "[f]or the primary task of reason is to cope consciously with the limitations imposed upon man by nature, is to fight against scarcity" (236).

If von Mises gives us the essential building blocks of the social cooperation suggested by the division of labor, it is Henry Hazlitt, in his great work *The Foundations of Morality,* who makes explicit what is only implicit in von Mises, namely, the ethical or moral nature of social cooperation. Indeed, for Hazlitt, the origins of morality are to be found in social cooperation or, what is essentially the same thing, the division of labor. "Every man, in his cool and rational moments, seeks his own long-run happiness. This is a *fact;* this is an *is.* Mankind has found, over the centuries, that certain rules of action best tend to promote the long-run happiness of both the individual and society. These rules of action have come to be called *moral* rules. Therefore, assuming that one seeks one's long-run happiness, these are the rules one *ought* to follow" (13). It is the very "oughtness" embedded in the "rules of action" and suggested by the individual's long-run interests that makes society possible. And to speak of "oughtness" is no more than to speak of ethics or morality. "[T]he whole of ethics rests upon the same foundation. For men find that they best promote their own interests in the long run not merely by refraining from injury to their fellows, but by cooperation with them. Social cooperation is the foremost means by which the majority of us attain most of our ends" (13). "And to recognize this leads us to recognize conduciveness to *social cooperation* as the great criterion of the rightness of actions, because voluntary social cooperation is the great means for the attainment not only of our collective but of nearly all our individual ends" (viii). For Hazlitt, therefore, there is no essential conflict or antithesis between the interests of the individual and the interests of society. "When the rightly understood interests of the individual are considered *in the long run,* they are found to be in harmony with and to *coincide* (almost if not to the point of identity) with the long-run interests of society" (viii). It is the rightly understood long-run interests of the individual that makes society possible and determines the nature of human activities, "[for] each individual is linked to his race by a tie, of all ties the strongest, the tie of self-regard" (85). This recognition, Hazlitt believes, is not only the foundation of morality but "the foundation of modern economics" (37). Thus, "[w]ithout social cooperation modern man could not achieve the barest fraction of the ends and satisfactions that he has achieved with it." "The very subsistence of the immense majority of us depends on it. We cannot treat subsistence as basely material and beneath our moral notice." (37).

All of this may seem to be an astronomically long distance from employee assistance, or it may seem to be much ado about nothing, or it may seem to be in the nature of an endurance contest for the reader, but there are, I believe, at least three good reasons for our seemingly circuitous route to our destination. First, contrary to what some people in the employee assistance field may think—especially those who are enamored of managed mental health care—employee assistance is more than a technical endeavor and more than the application of an assortment of techniques. That it is a technical endeavor encompassing a variety of techniques no one would deny, but it is also much more, for if what von Mises and Hazlitt are saying has any validity at all, it lies in their understanding of what the phrases "social cooperation" and "division of labor" mean. The alternative to social cooperation and the division of labor is, at best, a very menial existence and, at worst, chaos, probably widespread conflict, and, it goes without saying, the absence of anything we could even remotely call society. Absent would be most if not all of those conditions that men down through the ages have esteemed and even died for, conditions in which human dignity, self-respect, competence, to name just a few, have been prized and sought for precisely because they defined what it meant to be human. This is what von Mises means when he says that "[p]roduction is not something physical, material, and external; it is a spiritual and intellectual phenomenon" (103), or when he says that "[h]uman society is an intellectual and spiritual phenomenon" (145). He is speaking directly to the rational nature of man, and ultimately this is what employee assistance is all about. It is a recognition that the social bond can be and frequently is fragile and that endeavors to maintain and even enhance that bond contribute both to individual and social well-being. Admittedly, in the case of employee assistance, such efforts are by-products of attempts to resolve problem situations in the workplace, but ultimately all such efforts, from wherever they may emanate, tend towards the same end—the well-being of the individual and society.

Second, if there is one aspect of human nature that is conducive to the creation of problem situations, in the workplace or anywhere else, it is the propensity to take for granted those things—institutions, social structures, and human endeavors of all kinds—that in their apparent longevity and sheer facticity seem to possess the qualities of permanence and autonomy. It's as if they had always been there and would always be there, but nothing could be further from the truth. Whether we are talking about institutions that safeguard personal liberties or those that provide us with our material standard of living, they are all subject to decay, misrepresentation, and even manipulation. In short, to the degree that we take for granted those aspects of human nature that compel respect and those elements in our society and culture that make for social stability, to that degree we guarantee their demise. Perhaps another way of saying this is that society in all of its manifestations is, as Hazlitt so pointedly suggests, primarily a moral, not a technical endeavor. The question is essentially one of ends and only peripherally one of means.

Third, and this is to some extent a corollary of our second point, were it not for the highly ideological nature of much of what passes for social thought in our day and age, it would probably not be necessary to cite the works of scholars like von Mises and Hazlitt. Or if it were thought necessary to include them in the discussion it would be only to clarify certain key points, not the least of which is the primacy of reason in all human endeavors. Given, however, the very ideological nature of much of our social thought—whether the ideology is that of present-day movements such as multiculturalism, deconstructionism, certain varieties of feminism and environmentalism, and that old standby, socialism, or whether it was those variants of ideology present when von Mises and Hazlitt were writing, such as communism, National Socialism, and fascism—in which reason and the individual are denigrated in favor of a collectivist and emotionalist mysticism, it is, I believe, necessary to focus once again on those irreducible elements without which individual and social well-being are not possible. At the center of human activity is the human being who, possessed of the faculty of reason, works in concert with others to achieve her and their ends. To the possible objection that this has little or nothing to do with employee assistance, the response is that it has a great deal to do with employee assistance.

As noted earlier, apart from economics and its essential conceptual framework, employee assistance has little or no meaning; it is economics, and not psychology, that determines the nature and structure of employee assistance. It is concepts such as the division of labor, social cooperation, and productivity, and not therapy, that provide us with the surest foundation for implementing and maintaining effective employee assistance programs. It is not the therapist's or psychologist's office but the supervisor's office that is of paramount importance in the troubled employee's well-being, and it is not a diagnosis from the *DSM IV* but constructive confrontation that will move the employee to change her behavior. Were it not for the confusion surrounding much of what goes on under the heading of employee assistance none of this would have to be said.

All of this may appear to be no more than merely tangential to our discussion of employee assistance or even irrelevant, but given the profession's lack of focus, the abandonment of its basic principles, and the desire to be fashionable, it needs to be stated, over and over again if necessary, that employee assistance will not survive the loss of its roots in the worksite. The indisputable fact is that the profession has abandoned the worksite, and no amount of legerdemain can disguise or cover over the disastrous result of that abandonment. Chameleonlike, the profession today assumes whatever coloration the ideological environment dictates.

Whatever the fad of the moment is—whether it is managed mental health care, or clinical activities, or multiculturalism and diversity management, or social work, or any of a number of other trendy notions—one can be sure the profession will embrace it. Driven by the notion that change and innovation are synonyms for progress, the profession has jettisoned all criteria, standards, and principles and decided that it can be whatever one wishes to make it. To be sure, one can still find occasional references to the Core Technology in the literature, but only in passing; rarely, if ever, is there any kind of substantive discussion of the principles and practice of employee assistance. Within the context of present-day employee assistance practice, the Core Technology is of no more than antiquarian interest. Change, innovation, and progress are the leitmotifs of current employee assistance activities.

Were it not for the pernicious consequences of the doctrine that change and/or innovation equals progress, were those consequences, in other words, no more than an effort to improve or enhance the quality of employee assistance programs, the issue would be quite different. But for too many employee assistance practitioners, change, innovation, and progress have come to mean the abrogation of all standards, principles, and criteria. For these practitioners, prudence is not only not a virtue but rather an obstacle; because it suggests that at the very least we take a second look at whatever it is we are proposing to change or alter, prudence is deemed reactionary or, worse, irrelevant. For all of these reasons, it is necessary to restate the basic axioms or fundamental premises of employee assistance.

Our starting point is the division of labor, and here it is necessary to cite once more what is perhaps the basic axiom of von Mises's work: *"The fundamental social phenomenon is the division of labor and its counterpart human cooperation"* (italics added). Whatever else may be said about employee assistance, it is to the concept of the division of labor that everything that can be said about it must eventually be referred. Again, von Mises: "Experience teaches man that cooperative action is more efficient and productive than isolated action of self-sufficient individuals. The natural conditions determining man's life and effort are such that the division of labor increases output per unit of labor expended" (157–58). It is those "natural conditions determining man's life and effort" that are central to the development of society and social cooperation. To put this somewhat differently: Without the exploitation of those natural conditions to realize her ends, that is, the satisfaction of her needs and wants and a more satisfactory state of existence, society would not be possible. If people chose to be self-sufficient and live in isolation from their neighbors, there would not only be no society but perpetual conflict and open warfare for the possession of scarce goods. It would be literally a war of all against all. Thus it is natural necessity and the human capacity to grasp that necessity that dictates social cooperation. These are in the nature of immutable principles, and all efforts to contravene, subvert, or in any way deny that immutability will have disastrous consequences.

Whatever else it may be, the division of labor is a law of nature, inherent in the very structure of human nature and human endeavors and discoverable through the faculty of reason. It suggests to human beings the necessity of cooperation with others to improve the conditions of life for all. And this is also the basic axiom of employee assistance, for it is a fundamental assumption of the latter that social cooperation is the norm and that the troubled employee—whatever her behavior may be—is violating that norm, thus making social cooperation more difficult. To put this another way: If there were no troubled employees whose actions were making it difficult for themselves and others to attain agreed-upon ends, there would be no need for something called employee assistance. Employee assistance has its roots in the effort to enhance social cooperation by helping the troubled employee become, once again, a productive member of that society or community we call the worksite. Its effort is to help reestablish the norm of social cooperation. If the objection is that such a statement is obvious and needs no further elaboration, I would agree, were it not for the fact that this simple truth has been lost sight of by the profession in its haste to embrace the latest fad or trend.

Before we turn to the essential conceptual framework of employee assistance itself, it would be important, I believe, to draw a parallel between the concept of the division of labor and the role played by employee assistance in making the former and its counterpart, social cooperation, more effective. Just as the individual human being plays a major role in the communal effort to achieve agreed-upon ends, so too does an employee assistance program; its effort is analogous to that of the individual's in that it too must be an integral part of the institution it professes to serve and functioning effectively if social cooperation is to be a reality. This brings us to the idea of *integration,* an idea that is central to the concept of the division of labor and to employee assistance.

When we speak of employee assistance, the concept of integration is key to understanding the nature and structure of employee assistance. Thus we can say without fear of contradiction that an employee assistance program will be effective only to the degree that it is integrated into the larger organization—the company or institution—that it serves. Not understanding or misunderstanding this key concept leads, unfortunately, to the kinds of problems associated with the Carr-McCann version of employee assistance. Again, it is important to keep in mind that employee assistance is a creation of the worksite and that the latter, including its processes, procedures, and interdependencies—in other words, all of those things that collectively we call the division of labor—is its natural habitat. In an excellent essay on employee assistance, Charles A. Weaver develops the idea of integration to suggest the following: "An employee assistance program is a general term for a subsystem of interdependent components of the overall organizational system. It is a program for solving or reducing problems that affect the employee's acceptable job performance through the process of linking the employee with resources located within the community" (320). For Weaver, then, it is essential that an employee assistance program be an interdependent or fully integrated part of the "overall organizational system." Only when the EAP is fully integrated into the parent system will it be able to work effectively with the employee who is experiencing job performance problems. The reverse is also true: If it is not integrated into the overall organizational system, if it is not an interdependent part of the parent system, its effectiveness will be severely limited. Thus when Weaver describes employee assistance as "a general term for a subsystem of interdependent components of the overall organizational system," he is suggesting that the EAP, the supervisor, and the institution, working together as an integrated system, can provide the troubled employee with a highly effective resource capable of returning him to full productivity. This is what Weaver means when he states that: "*Systems* theory is implied in developing employee assistance programs. Systems theory assumes an agency or other social organization consists of an interdependent set of activities composed of subsystems that function within the larger set of parent institution and community. The step-by-step approach to EAP development (e.g., beginning with assessing management commitment and proceeding through implementation to evaluation) represents a systems approach. Each component affects the other components and the overall program affects the organization. The organization, in turn, affects the community. Careful analysis of the key factors affecting the system is essential to employee assistance program development" (323).

What Weaver is suggesting here is that the best way to understand employee assistance conceptually and practically is through systems theory, which states, in effect, (1) that all of the component parts of a system are reciprocally influential, and, therefore, (2) a change in one part of the system will affect every other part of the system and the system as a whole. Weaver is also suggesting, implicitly at least, that if the EAP is not integrated into the parent system to the degree that it exerts a beneficial influence on the worksite, its voice will not be authoritative within the community that is the worksite and may indeed even be detrimental to the purposes of the division of labor inherent in the EAP's status as a subsystem within the overall system. It will not, in other words, contribute much to the social cooperation necessary to achieve the ends implied in the division of labor and may, inadvertently and by default, subvert those ends.

Thus, when Weaver speaks of "the key factors affecting the system," he is suggesting that the legitimacy of the employee assistance program rests exclusively on the degree to which these key factors are present and substantive. If they are not in place, the *authority* of the EAP, which is derived exclusively from the well-defined *function* it serves (or should serve) as a subsystem within the larger system, will be suspect at best.

This last point needs to be emphasized over and over again; indeed, it cannot be stressed too much or too often, for far too many employee assistance programs are such in name only. The function they are designed to realize is absent or in some way handicapped because they are not an integral part of the institutions they purport to serve. As function goes, so goes authority.

The issues of legitimacy and authority are also the reasons why Weaver stresses the importance of assessing management (and especially, I would add, executive management) commitment to the EAP (a "key factor") as a logical and necessary first step. In all too many instances, employee assistance programs are implemented without adequate knowledge on the part of management about the nature, structure, and purpose of employee assistance, or to meet a momentary or temporary need and then eliminated or relegated to a kind of stepchild status once the moment or need has passed. If management is not thoroughly committed to and knowledgeable about the principles and practice of employee assistance, the EAP will not survive or at best it will function in a limited way. It is the case, then, that the issues of legitimacy and authority—the former born of its systemic status and the latter corresponding to the function it serves—are of primary importance if the EAP is to function effectively and achieve its ends. This is also why it is complete nonsense to talk about "some type of employee assistance."

"EAPs Are *Worksite-based* Programs," a short but incisive essay in the *Metro/EAP News* for March 1997 makes this point clearly by linking the concept of employee assistance as worksite-based with the concept of employee assistance as an integrated subsystem within a larger system: "The term 'worksite-based' is critical to the EAP definition. This term does not mean that an EAP is internal with salaried staff in the traditional sense of that term. Instead, this term assigns ownership of the program and its goals to the company, not the vendor . . . Worksite-based also means the EAP interacts internally with a multi-faceted set of services based upon the core technology that allows it to serve as a management tool to influence a healthy bottom line. An EAP exists by way of company policies, procedures, and guidelines. . . . EAPs are not sold to the company like a payroll or custodial service (although many EAPs that *fail to integrate* with the organization match this description)" (1, italics added).

The only disagreement I have with the author of the essay is the use of the term "worksite-based" rather than the more specific and definitive phrase "worksite-based management program." Although the author does describe the EAP as a "management tool" and states that it is the company that owns the program and its goals, neither the idea that it is a management tool nor the notion of company ownership of the program can be derived from the term "worksite-based." The most that the latter can signify is that employee assistance activities take place in the work-site, not who or what owns the program. Moreover, deleting the word "management" from the definition of employee assistance places the company and management at one remove from the EAP, thereby con-tributing to the confusion surrounding management's and especially the supervisor's role in identifying the troubled employee. Put another way: Defining employee assistance as worksite-based only dilutes the ideas of accountability and responsibility and leaves them in a kind of limbo— no one knows for sure who is minding the store, and this is the source of many of the problems outlined by the author of the essay. In other words, the idea of integration—so essential to an effective EAP—is not conveyed by the term "worksite-based." The essential point is this: To define employee assistance as worksite-based only is to exclude by def-inition anyone's ownership of the program, except perhaps that of the EAP professional. Definitions are meaningful only to the degree that they suggest what is inclusive and exclusive to the object in question.

The author of the essay is, however, on solid ground when he states that an employee assistance program will be effective when, and only when, the company is the owner of the program, because it is only when the company owns the program that it will be integrated as an authori-tative subsystem within the parent system. But it is also necessary to point out that only if the program is integrated into the company structure will it be owned by the company. In this sense, ownership and integration are synonymous. (And this, parenthetically, is why the association's pre-vious name, ALMACA, was more conducive to company ownership of the program than the present name, EAPA. An association of labor-management administrators and consultants is inclusive, suggesting as it does a joint communal effort to resolve problem situations in the work-place, while an association of employee assistance professionals sug-gests, implicitly at least, that the experts are to be found only in the professional organization. Perhaps another way of saying this is that su-pervisors and union representatives have as much to contribute to the resolution of problem situations in the workplace as does the EAP professional.)

Paul Roman makes much the same point about integration in an article entitled "All EA Functions Should Be Internal" in *Employee Assistance* for March 1994. In it, he asks and answers a question: "What is meant by an internal program? Very simply, an activity that is integrated into organizational structure and functioning. Something that is permanent and represents the standard way of dealing with a certain set of issues, i.e., troubled employees" (10). And for Roman also, it makes little difference whether the program is located in-house or out-of-house; what is important is that the program is "integrated into organizational structure and functioning." The EAP, if it is to be effective, must have a taken-for-granted quality within the organization, just as much so as any other integral part of the organization. "Employee Assistance" and "the employee assistance program" should be as familiar to employees throughout the organization and at every level of the organization as, for example, the human resources or the employee benefits department. This is what Roman means when he states that the EAP should be "[s]omething that is permanent and represents the standard way of dealing with a certain set of issues, i.e., troubled employees." But implementing and maintaining an employee assistance program is a process that is educational in nature and involves several steps, all of which are essential and each of which represents a necessary building block in the development of effective employee assistance programs.

The first, and in many ways the most important step in integrating the employee assistance program into the company structure, is evaluating the commitment of executive management to the program through the development of a policy statement. Largely ignored in today's entrepreneurial environment, the policy statement is fundamental, for two reasons: (1) the development of a policy statement will indicate the depth and scope of management's commitment to the program; and (2) it is the first of several integrative steps necessary to insure the success of the program. The policy statement should be both detailed and comprehensive, indicating clearly why the program is being implemented, that it has the full support of management, including executive management, that supervisors at all levels are responsible for implementing and carrying out the provisions of the policy, that the impetus for the program is the organization's concern for its employees, and that the program is an integral and authoritative element in the structure of the organization and enjoys the same status as any other department or division of the organization. To skip this step or to attempt to implement a policy statement that is less than clear and specific will only insure an ineffective program. Weaver describes the policy statement as "essential": "While the policy and procedure statement do not insure the existence of a program, they are essential to effective programs. Well-designed, publicized statements of policy and procedures can provide momentum for EAPs" (329–30). As Weaver suggests, the policy should not only be well designed but it should be publicized; every employee of the company should receive a copy of the policy statement and an orientation to its purpose. Weaver outlines fourteen points that he believes should be present in any policy statement:

1 The recognized need for the program.
2 Support for the program from both management and labor.
3 The willingness of the organization to commit time and resources to the EAP.
4 Accessible points of contact for employee assistance and procedures to follow.
5 An acceptable attitude about mental illness, alcoholism, and family/marital problems.
6 A concern by the organization for its employees.
7 The scope of the problems to be covered by the EAP.
8 The target group for the EAP.
9 Job security and promotional opportunities of those participating in the program.
10 Confidentiality of records.
11 Job performance as the basis for supervisory recommendations.
12 The voluntary nature of the program.
13 Sick leave and insurance benefits.
14 The relationship to other personnel and administrative policies.

Although all of Weaver's 14 points are essential to a clear and comprehensive policy statement, the last is crucial if the EAP is to be fully integrated into the structure of the institution, for if the EAP policy statement does not have the same kind of significance and status as other institutional policy statements, neither will the EAP have the same kind of significance and status as other components of the organization. If the policy statement is viewed as no more than a kind of add-on or afterthought or relegated to a kind of stepchild status within the organization, so too will the employee assistance program itself. Farmer and Maynard put it this way: "EAP-related policy statements should always be presented as one of the basic company personnel policies. The format and style in which they are written should conform to the format and style in which other company policy statements are written. Company corrective, disciplinary, and grievance procedures should be revised to incorporate the EAP into them; EAP-related practices should not be described separately as if they were simply grafted on to the basic procedures as an afterthought" (34). Again, the key concept, as it is when establishing or implementing all of the essential components of an EAP, is integration. Failure to integrate even one of the key elements of an employee assistance program will insure its ineffectiveness and probably its failure. Needless to say, the presence of a policy statement will not guarantee the success of a program, but its absence will almost certainly guarantee its failure. Without the support of management, especially executive management, an employee assistance program will founder.

As noted above, employee assistance had its origins in the worksite and its functions circumscribed and defined by the worksite. Building on what von Mises and Hazlitt describe as the division of labor and human cooperation, it remains now to explore, at least briefly, the nature of the worksite or, more precisely, what it is that sets the worksite apart from other kinds of endeavors or institutions and suggests the role that a well-implemented employee assistance program can play in contributing to the effectiveness of the worksite and greater productivity.

When we think of the worksite, or "work," what comes to mind is a place, a location, or an environment where people pursue an occupation or a career of some kind and for the performance of the duties associated with that occupation or career receive remuneration of some kind, usually in the form of wages and benefits. In this sense, a worksite may be a manufacturing plant or a hospital, and it may be a small one-owner one-employee business, a farm, or a large corporation employing thousands of people. Whatever its size or purpose, the worksite, like other institutions, is characterized by a high degree of human interaction and human interdependence, but unlike some institutions, it is also characterized by a high degree of functionality, abstraction, and rationalization or standardization, all of which overlap with and influence one another. Perhaps another way of saying this is that the worksite is instrumental, that is, based on reason, rather than affectional, as is, for example, the family.

Although it would be too much to say that the worksite is impersonal, it is the case that personal relationships are subordinated to the functional requirements of the organization—this is not to deny that close and long-term relationships do begin and flourish in the worksite—requirements such as the elaboration and extension of processes, the codification of responsibilities, including the contractual or semi-contractual nature of relationships (more about this later), and planning. The quest is for efficiency, and generally, and with some few exceptions, personal idiosyncrasies are rarely encouraged or tolerated. The functional requirements of the organization take precedence.

A high degree of abstraction is also characteristic of the worksite. Successful companies constantly review and improve processes and procedures, refine manufacturing, service and marketing strategies and techniques, and upgrade the skills of their employees. Successful companies are very much aware that their continued success demands constant evaluation and reevaluation of all of their efforts, from those that are merely peripheral to the main business of the company, such as compliance with a morass of federal, state, and local regulations, to those that have the greatest impact on the continued financial health of the company, such as technological change and innovation.

Finally, the rationalization or standardization of processes, procedures, and behaviors is central to the continued efficient functioning of an institution, for one major reason if for no other: The organization—any organization—is essentially a system, and since it is a system, its various component parts must be functioning in such a way that they complement one another and the system as a whole. Without a high degree of standardization or rationalization, very few companies would survive for any period of time.

Thus, functionality, abstraction, and rationalization or standardization are inherent in and intrinsic to the structure and purpose of the worksite and suggest its end or purpose, that for which it was created to accomplish or satisfy. These are the *normative requirements* of the organization, and absent these normative requirements or inherent qualities, there would be no need for something called employee assistance, and absent the capacity of employee assistance to help maintain or support these requirements, employee assistance would have no meaning. And this is also the reason why the notion of "some type of employee assistance" is utterly without meaning; unless employee assistance is knowledgeable about, attentive to, and capable of responding to the subtle as well as not-so-subtle dynamics of the worksite, it will be ineffective. Another way of saying this is that employee assistance does not attempt to impose or superimpose principles, processes, or procedures that are alien or extraneous to the structure and purpose of an organization, nor does it suggest that the ends or purposes of the organization be subordinated to the ends or purposes of employee assistance. Neither is it, nor should it be, a kind of external vendor selling an add-on product or a kind of part-time or on-call consulting service whose presence is requested only when crises occur. It should, rather, have a permanent and visible presence within the institution, and in order to have those qualities *it must be integrated into and a function of the normative requirements of the institution.* It must, in other words, work with and within those processes and procedures that are intrinsic to and inherent in the structure and purpose of the organization and that call for a high degree of cooperation and interdependence, not only within the organization but also between the latter and external entities, such as suppliers or vendors and, of course, customers. It is, then, the nature of the organization—its ability to create and integrate specific behaviors with clearly delineated processes and procedures—that dictates the activities of employee assistance. Those behaviors, processes, and procedures constitute, in effect, the normative requirements of the institution. And it is from these normative requirements that employee assistance, in turn, derives its basic and essential principles. Absent these normative requirements, employee assistance would have no meaning; there would be no structure or context within which employee assistance could carry out its essential mission—that of assisting the organization in identifying early on and confronting constructively the troubled employee on the basis of impaired job performance, or, in Paul Roman's words, resolving "a quite wide range of problem situations in the workplace." Here, in miniature, as it were, is what von Mises and Hazlitt mean when they speak of the division of labor or social cooperation—that which is the foundation of the economic system and that which provides the most general or the broadest context for the activities of employee assistance.

But it is at this point that employee assistance faces a formidable obstacle—whether the program is in-house or out-of-house, it must, in order to be integrated into the institution, demonstrate its ability to be a function of the normative requirements of the latter, but in order to function in that capacity it must be integrated into the institution. Moreover, the process is not a single event or something that is over and done with once the program is implemented; what is important in this respect is implementation *and* maintenance, an ongoing and continual process of education and communication with employees, supervisors, and executive management. This is why Paul Roman and others stress over and over again the importance of continuing education and communication if the program is to have that integral and taken-for-granted quality that is absolutely necessary if it is to be effective. Since communication and education are the sine qua non of effective employee assistance programs, they cannot be overemphasized.

This is also the reason why managed mental health care is incompatible with and even inimical to the basic principles of employee assistance. Simply put, managed mental health care has no interest in the normative requirements of the institution and, indeed, sees those requirements as obstacles to its professed end—the reduction of costs associated with mental health care and the profits entailed in doing so. For if employee assistance is—as Paul Roman suggests, and I believe correctly—a mechanism for the resolution of problem situations in the workplace, then it is the resolution of those problem situations, and not the direct short-term costs of behavioral health care, that must be the focus of employee assistance. The rationale, of course, is that resolving those problem situations will increase productivity, thereby decreasing costs in the long term. Moreover, when managed mental health care denies or restricts services in order to reduce costs, it is almost a certain guarantee that many if not most of those problem situations will be exacerbated, thereby increasing costs in the long term. In other words, employee assistance takes a systemic view of the worksite and its long-term activities and consequences—all of which come under the heading of organizational development—while managed mental health care has no interest in the worksite as a system or as the focus of efforts to help the troubled employee and sees only the short-term financial consequences. Another way of saying this is that employee assistance understands cost savings—or what is the same thing, increased productivity—as a by-product of resolving problem situations in the workplace. The different ends or purposes of employee assistance and managed mental health care constitute sufficient reason to question the alleged compatibility of the two. We will examine this issue in a great deal more detail in Part III.

None of this—systems theory, institutional requirements, or employee assistance as a "mechanism"—is intended to suggest that people are merely automatons in a kind of abstract mechanical system devoid of human purpose, energy, or creativity. Quite the contrary—it is people who implement and direct the system, maintain it, and, when necessary, change it. Thus it is people, and not abstractions, who will make or break a system. Unlike those who believe that human beings are merely products of their environment or no more than helpless pawns in the grip of the iron laws of history or the contingencies of the moment, employee assistance suggests not only that people are initiators and creators but also that they are capable of change fundamentally and lastingly. In fact, it is only on the basis of this truth that von Mises and Hazlitt can speak of the division of labor and social cooperation, for if these have any meaning at all it is that human beings *voluntarily* come together to accomplish ends that would be difficult if not impossible to accomplish in isolation.

It is within this context only that we are better able to understand the troubled employee whose job performance is less than adequate, since it is only within this context, that is, a systems context based on voluntary social cooperation, that we can understand the troubled employee as not merely a troubled employee whose job performance problems exist in isolation, but as an employee whose job performance problems are affecting others, especially his supervisor and coworkers. The problem is systemic in that she adversely affects not only company processes and procedures but other people as well. It is the "pebble in the pond" idea; the troubled employee whose job performance is deteriorating sends out ripples that can and frequently do affect others and in some instances an entire company. (Several years ago I worked with an employee whose job performance problems paralyzed a company of 160 employees.) The old adage that if you have a troubled employee you have a troubled supervisor is accurate.

This is also the reason why Weaver suggests "assessing management commitment" when developing an employee assistance program and why he believes that "an employee assistance program is a general term for a subsystem of interdependent components of the overall organizational system." If the EAP is not a subsystem within the larger system, that is, if it is not a vital and integral part of the system, or if it is not understood by management or not understood by management to be such, then it simply will not function or at least not function as well as it could and should. There will be little or no understanding of the system as a system, or of the system as a complex entity guided and governed by the cooperation of those who comprise the system, or of the role the employee assistance program could and should be playing in contributing to the resolution of problem situations in the system. On many occasions during my tenure in the field, I've heard employee assistance practitioners lament the fact that management does not understand what it is they are trying to do, or, more frequently, that supervisors are not using the program. Until management—and here again I must emphasize the essential role of executive management—has a sure grasp of what employee assistance is and what it is designed to do, or until it is thoroughly integrated into the parent system—ultimately the two are the same—the laments will continue to be heard. This, again, is why the Carr-McCann notion of offering employers "some type of employee assistance" makes very little sense. Since there is no context, no system of relationships, and, apparently, no regard for the dynamics of interdependencies, how is anyone to know what it is or what it is supposed to do? How are employers and employees to use it? Carr and McCann simply ignore or are unaware of the normative requirements of the institution.

Chapter 5

EMPLOYEE ASSISTANCE AND THE ROLE OF MANAGEMENT

The overriding importance of management's role in understanding, implementing, and maintaining employee assistance programs has already been indicated, but it cannot be emphasized too much. Without management's approval and understanding, an employee assistance program will founder. It may assume the role of an outside vendor, which, while offering legitimate employee assistance services, remains in limbo because it is not integrated into the company—it is not the company's program. As Charles Weaver suggests: "[C]areful analysis of the key factors affecting the system is essential to employee assistance program development." And what could be more of a key factor or more important than management in insuring the success of the program?

The role of management in implementing and maintaining employee assistance programs must be emphasized over and over again, if for no other reason than that even those who are committed to traditional EAP principles and practice, including the Core Technology, do not see the forest for the trees. In a short unsigned essay entitled "Myth No[.] 1: EAPs Are Part of the Employee Benefit Package" in the *Metro/EAP News* for March 1997, the author states the following: "EAPs are not part of a company's fringe benefits package and are probably misrepresented, or are not EAPs, if portrayed as such. Although EAPs have a beneficial impact on employee health and productivity, they are pro-people and pro-organization management tools. The misunderstanding of EAPs as 'employee benefits' has resulted from a re-definition of EAPs in popular health care and managed care literature, which has displaced traditional core technology-based articles. . . . Since the assessment and referral functions of EAPs (a frequently unbundled service sold to many companies) [have] proven useful when inter-mingled with managed care, these so-called EAPs without *active* core technology elements appear to the uninformed as simply part of the benefits package" (3). The central point in this paragraph—that EAPs are not part of the employee's benefit package—is correct. And there is no question that the intermingling of employee assistance and managed mental health care has been disastrous for the field. The author mentions also that EAPs "are pro-people and pro-organization management tools," which is the case. The problem, however, is that this description could easily entail the notion that EAPs are indeed part of the benefits package and therefore no more than an employee benefit. When the author states that EAPs "are pro-people and pro-organization management tools," he is, as I suggested, correct, but what precisely does "pro-people and pro-organization management tools" mean? What is the end or purpose of these "tools"? Employee benefits are also, after all, pro-people and pro-organization management tools. The author fails to distinguish clearly the nature and purpose of employee assistance from the nature and purpose of employee compensation. Moreover, when we read the entire sentence—"Although EAPs have a beneficial impact on employee health and productivity, they are pro-people and pro-organization management tools"—the confusion is compounded. Implicitly at least, the sentence appears to set at odds the notion of, on the one hand, "a beneficial impact on employee health and productivity" with, on the other, the notion that "they are pro-people and pro-organization management tools." At the very least, the sentence leaves the impression that the two ideas are distinctly different. Then too, the sentence could easily be interpreted to read that employee health and productivity are not central to employee assistance since the latter is a pro-people and pro-organization management tool, which also makes very little sense. What, exactly, is the distinction between employee assistance and an employee benefits package? More to the point, perhaps, what does it mean to say that an employee assistance program is a pro-people and pro-organization management tool? Although the author's effort to distinguish between employee benefits and employee assistance is commendable, it ultimately obscures rather than enlightens.

The issue—and here I must contend with the author of the essay, not so much for a sin of commission as for one of omission—is that employee assistance professionals themselves have contributed to the confusion. As I noted in Chapter 3, EAPA has been derelict in safeguarding the core of employee assistance doctrine by omitting the word "management" from its definition of employee assistance. To define employee assistance as only a "worksite-based program," and not as a "worksite-based management program," is to deprive employee assistance of one of its principal mainstays. Definitions are crucial to understanding, not just for establishing boundaries—what is included and what is not included in the entity under consideration—but also for indicating the essential elements or components of the thing being defined. When EAPA omitted the single most important element—management—from its definition of an employee assistance program, it deposited the latter in limbo and made it an easy target for the entrepreneur. Within the context of the present EAPA definition, why couldn't an employee benefit package be defined as employee assistance? And when the author of the essay cited above states that EAPs are pro-people and pro-organization management tools, he is, as I suggested, correct, but the question remains: Who or what grounds the EAP in the worksite? To reiterate: It is the troubled employee whose job performance is inadequate or deteriorating who is the central focus of employee assistance, and this focus, of necessity, brings management front and center and distinguishes employee assistance from employee benefits packages where the focus is on compensation. It is the active engagement of the supervisor with the troubled employee, within a context that is defined and circumscribed by management and that is based on the principles of early identification of the troubled employee on the basis of impaired job performance and constructive confrontation, which defines employee assistance and distinguishes it from employee compensation, human resources, and other activities that fall within the range of the human services.

A layperson, trying to understand the present EAPA definition, would no doubt be perplexed. He might assume that an employee assistance program is an employee benefit, perhaps a counseling program designed to help employees who have personal problems, but he could assume no more. He would have no idea of who or what, except perhaps the employee assistance practitioner, is the principle mainstay of the EAP in the worksite. Thus the absence of management from EAPA's definition of employee assistance accomplishes exactly the same thing as Carr and McCann accomplish with their notion of "some type of employee assistance"—it leaves employee assistance rudderless.

Perhaps another way of saying this is that while the worksite defines the boundaries and indicates the focus of employee assistance, it is management that provides the impetus and the incentive, if you will, the vital principle for the program. Without management's understanding that it is the prime mover in an employee assistance program, and without direct and vigorous management involvement and participation in the program, employee assistance will remain no more than a kind of employee benefit. If employee assistance professionals are uncomfortable with the inroads managed mental health care has made into the profession, if they are perplexed about the existence today of employee assistance programs that are no more than fronts—a kind of camouflage—for managed mental health care programs, and if they are less than happy with the erosion of employee assistance principles and practice over the past fifteen years or so, they need look no further than themselves for the causes. It is more than mere coincidence that management disappeared in the employee assistance scheme of things when ALMACA disappeared in the late 1980s.

The worksite, then, is the focus of employee assistance, and management the active principle, and these facts carry several implications. First, it suggests that it is the dynamics of the worksite—the relationships, interactions, and behaviors of people in the worksite—that constitute the central focus of employee assistance. It is not the employee in isolation nor is it even employee personal problems that are of primary concern for employee assistance; it is, rather, the physical, intellectual, and moral forces, which produce and govern all that takes place in the worksite, that are the proper and legitimate concern of the employee assistance practitioner. Not understanding this is a major reason for the failure of so many EAPs. Second, the focus on the worksite as the context for EAP activity also suggests that employee assistance must be management oriented, for it is management at all levels that determines the nature, structure, and evolution of worksite interactions, relationships, and behavior. This is not to say that employees do not contribute to activities in the worksite—they do, even to the extent of improving or enhancing processes and procedures—but merely to indicate that employee activities take place within boundaries determined by the nature of the work and management prescription. Third, the focus on the worksite and management's role in prescribing the kinds of activities that take place within the worksite suggest the consultation function of employee assistance—a function that permits management and the EAP consultant to work together to resolve problem situations in the worksite. When management knows that it can—and indeed is obliged to—consult with the EAP about a particular problem or problems related to employee performance, it is much more likely to do so. Fourth, an employee assistance program that is integrated into the organization will be one that is focused on the worksite and will be, consequently, a fully and competently functioning component of the organization. And herein lies one of the fundamental aspects of employee assistance—to the degree that it is integrated into the organizational structure of the institution, to that degree it can contribute to both the short-term and long-term goals of the organization. Finally, and perhaps most importantly, the focus on the worksite permits the EAP, in conjunction with management, to respond to a wide variety of problem situations in the workplace. But to say this is no more than to repeat in different words the basic axiom of Ludwig von Mises's work: "The fundamental social phenomenon is the division of labor and its counterpart human cooperation."

In order to illustrate concretely the issues involved in denying the importance of management's role in employee assistance, I have found it useful to think in terms of two employee assistance "models" (asking the reader to bracket temporarily the fact that to speak of models, plural, is a contradiction) that, for the sake of convenience and illustration, I call the "employee benefit" model and the "management program" model, the latter the traditional model embracing the Core Technology. Comparing and contrasting the two models will suggest strongly that the employee benefit model is not employee assistance at all but merely a kind of counseling program that has no necessary or contingent relationship to employee assistance, rightly understood, and that in fact is inimical to the latter.

The basic principles of the employee benefit model are two: (1) it is essentially a counseling program that is (2) based on self-referral or what is called voluntary referral, which in turn presumes self-identification on the part of the employee. He becomes aware that some problem or situation is impinging upon his ability to function competently as a person or as an employee or both, at which point he contacts the employee assistance program and is assessed and counseled or referred for counseling. There may even be an occasional supervisor referral to the EAP, but such referrals are rare and usually made only after a crisis of some magnitude has occurred. Moreover, there may even be supervisor training of some sort in the employee benefit model, but is usually perfunctory in nature (more of an orientation than training) and tacitly or otherwise sends the clear message to supervisors and management that employee assistance is primarily an employee benefit and thus outside the mainstream of corporate training and management practice. The result, very frequently, is confusion on the part of supervisors about the nature and purpose of employee assistance. The supervisor then does indeed become isolated and frequently at a loss as to how to approach an employee whose job performance is deteriorating or whose absenteeism is increasing. Put another way: To view employee assistance as only or primarily an employee benefit is to deny the degree to which it can enhance supervisory skills and boost productivity and, ultimately, to consign the program to a marginal role within the company.

If these were the only or the most serious problems attendant upon viewing employee assistance as only or primarily an employee benefit, we might, with some justification, argue that more people are getting help than would be the case if the EAP did not exist at all. That view is accurate; few people would suggest that employee assistance-as-employee benefit does not help people. It does. The problem, however, is that the less than satisfactory consequences of the employee benefit model outlined above are neither the most serious nor the most damaging consequences of the model. There are other and potentially more serious flaws in the employee assistance-as-employee benefit model.

First and foremost, the employee benefit model will not reach very many of those employees who are experiencing an alcohol or drug problem or a serious emotional problem, except in rare instances, and then only when, as noted earlier, a crisis of major import has occurred. The hallmark of these illnesses is denial, and in the absence of a mechanism for early identification and confrontation (again, Roman's mechanism "for the resolution of a quite wide range of problem situations in the workplace"), these employees will get progressively worse, their work performance will continue to deteriorate, and, ultimately, they will be terminated or resign. In many, perhaps most, of these instances, the supervisor is aware of the employee's declining job performance and is even knowledgeable about the employee's personal problem, but because the EAP is viewed primarily as an employee benefit, the supervisor declines to take action until the problem can no longer be ignored. This is a situation I've seen played out over and over again during my tenure in the field and continue to see, all because the employee assistance program was not integrated into the organizational structure. Management was absent.

Second, the employee assistance-as-employee benefit model, by the very nature of its perception of employee assistance, eschews ongoing consultation with supervisors and managers, thus reinforcing in the latter the idea that employee assistance is no more than an employee benefit. There appears to be little or no understanding that the supervisor is the key agent in the functioning of an EAP and that his presence or absence will determine to a very great degree the effectiveness of the program.

Finally, and this may be the least apparent but one of the most important consequences of slighting the role of management in employee assistance programs, the absence of management has the effect of obscuring the worksite as the context for employee assistance. And without a clearly defined context, that is, without a clearly defined role for management—the two are almost synonymous—it is difficult if not impossible to see and understand relationships (social cooperation), to locate necessary referents (authority), and to provide a foundation for practice (principles, processes, and procedures). All we are left with is a number of isolated entities that have no apparent relationship to one another and provide little or no direction for what it is we are attempting to understand or do. It has been well said that ours is an age awash in facts and diminished in understanding. Perhaps another way of saying this is that when we deny or minimize the role of management in employee assistance programs, the worksite as the context for such programs becomes irrelevant, because now the entire burden of identifying and confronting inadequate job performance becomes the sole responsibility of the troubled employee himself. The employee, in effect, is placed in the position of supervising himself with little or no support from management.

If we could abstract from what has been said above about the consequences of the employee assistance-as-employee benefit model of employee assistance, we would arrive at the following:

1. the EAP exists on the margins of the organization; there is little or no supervisor involvement in the EAP, hence little or no consultation between the EAP and management;

2. there is little or no substantive supervisor training, especially the kind of training that emphasizes early identification of impaired job performance and constructive confrontation of the impaired employee;

3. there are fewer alcohol and drug referrals and fewer referrals of employees with serious emotional problems; and

4. the emphasis is on counseling and/or treatment.

In contrast to the employee assistance-as-employee benefit model of employee assistance is the employee assistance-as-management program model, a model that incorporates the concepts of early identification and constructive confrontation of the troubled employee. Indeed, as soon as we mention early identification and constructive confrontation, we are explicitly assuming that the EAP is integral to the management process; it follows logically and of necessity that when a supervisor identifies declining job performance and moves to correct it, he is engaging in standard management practice and not something that is ancillary to or other than "real" management practice. This is the key concept in the implementation and development of an effective employee assistance program. In their *Spirits and Demons at Work: Alcohol and Other Drugs on the Job*, Paul Roman and Harrison Trice make this point clearly: "Supervisors, at all levels, can make or break the effectiveness of constructive confrontation. They alone are in a position to identify impairment and such identification is clearly part of their normal scope of responsibility" (175). Put another way: Implied in the phrase "management program" is an important concept that is frequently ignored or overlooked in employee assistance programs, namely, that a well-implemented program will be at the very center of the management process since the skills it emphasizes—early identification of inadequate job performance and constructive confrontation of the troubled employee— are basic and essential supervisory/management skills. Thus it is with the knowledge and possession of these skills within a context that legitimizes and authorizes their use that the supervisor can be effective. This, again, is the "mechanism" Roman speaks of and the reason why a definition of employee assistance that omits the word management is less than adequate. The key word is integration—integration of the EAP into the management process; anything less than complete integration creates uncertainty on the part of supervisors about the nature and purpose of employee assistance.

What does all of this mean for supervisors and those they supervise? First, when supervisors understand employee assistance as a legitimate and authoritative subsystem within the larger system—as legitimate and authoritative as, say, human resources—there is less likelihood that they will shy away from or postpone dealing with impaired job performance on the part of those they supervise. Unfortunately, it is too often the case that supervisors, in the absence of an EAP, or in the case of a poorly implemented one, will feel isolated from any source of support for their efforts or feel inadequate to the task of maintaining job standards. The issue of supervisor isolation is an all too common one. When, however, supervisors know that the employee assistance program is there to support their efforts, there is a much greater probability that they will deal directly and much more quickly with troubling individuals and situations, thereby diminishing the potential for crisis. Supervisor understanding of the employee assistance program and the context in which it functions are necessary conditions for effective management and for effective use of the program.

Second, employees—especially those employees whose personal problems are impairing their job performance—also benefit when the EAP is a thoroughly integrated part of institutional and management processes.

Since it is much more likely in such a program that aberrant behavior or poor work performance will be confronted more quickly by the supervisor, it is also more likely that the troubled employee, sooner rather than later, will get the help he needs. To reiterate, this is crucially important for the employee who may be suffering from an alcohol or drug problem or a serious emotional problem.

In view of the importance of the concepts of early identification of impaired job performance and constructive confrontation to an effective employee assistance program, it is difficult to understand why some writers downplay the mandatory or supervisor referral. Wright states that if a company decides to implement an EAP through his agency (the Family Service Association of Toronto), "the company must adopt the voluntary referral, but we offer the suggested and mandatory referrals as a choice to be decided upon by the committee" (18). It is difficult to know what to make of this statement, but if it means what it appears to mean, then it is merely another instance of the employee assistance-as-employee benefit model, which has all of the deficiencies outlined above, especially the tendency to minimize the importance of a mechanism for confronting denial and rationalization. Moreover, it is not at all clear what Wright means by a "voluntary" referral, but if he means self-referral, then there is the obvious question: Why would an organization implement an employee assistance program that does not incorporate mandatory or supervisor referrals as an essential component of the program? This is almost like saying that a human resource department without the ability or authority to screen and interview job applicants would still be a human resource department; it might, but one would be justified in questioning its purpose and effectiveness. And what does Wright mean when he talks about "suggested and mandatory referrals"? Are these the same, or are there differences between the two? Also, what is the difference between a voluntary and a suggested referral? Wright's statement also raises another important question: If a company decides to adopt only the voluntary referral, does this mean that an employee could be terminated for poor job performance without a referral to the EAP? Implicitly at least, it would seem so.

Elsewhere, Wright suggests that "if, in the normal administration of discipline, a supervisor has reason to believe that the employee has a personal problem that may be contributing to his poor performance, the supervisor may suggest that the employee arrange for an interview with the employee assistance counselor" (19). The question, obviously, is: Why must the supervisor have "reason to believe" that the employee has a personal problem before suggesting a visit to the EAP? To put this question a slightly different way: What happens in those cases where an employee's job performance is impaired but the supervisor does not have reason to believe that the employee has a personal problem? Would this mean that the supervisor would not suggest a referral to the EAP?

All of this is simply to muddy the waters and signals, as Roman and Trice suggest, "the impending displacement of work-based programs by relatively vague strategies of counseling and treatment" (xvii). It also signals the importance of understanding employee assistance as a worksite-based management program, that is, as a program that is a well-integrated part of the management and organizational processes.

Perhaps the best approach to understanding employee assistance-as-management program is the concept of contract. Here again Roman and Trice are instructive: "Because impaired performance violates the fundamental contract between employer and employees, there is a legitimate right to intervene and offer constructive help" (xiv). Insofar as there is an integral relationship between supervisors and the employee assistance program, the notion of contract mediates that relationship and legitimizes both the supervisor's role and the role of the employee assistance program. Whether written or unwritten, formal or informal, a contract exists between employer and employee, and "contract" means no more and no less than that of acquiring or incurring obligations. Thus the concept of contract implies, on the one hand, reciprocity, a mutual exchange of benefits and/or privileges and, on the other hand, sanctions, which are penalties for noncompliance. Speaking of the sanctions present in the strategy of constructive confrontation, Roman and Trice suggest that they "do not stem from a moralistic view, but rather are a legitimate part of the employer-employee contract" (178–79). The right of the supervisor to intervene, then, in cases of impaired job performance, is legitimized by the existence of a contract between employers and employees. And it is also the existence of that contract that provides the rationale for the existence of employee assistance programs. This stands in sharp contrast to the employee assistance-as-employee benefit approach, which ignores the supervisor and the extraordinary potential of the worksite for confronting and modifying disruptive behavior. Roman and Trice sum the matter up this way: "The work place provides a relationship that is relatively personal but characterized by a legitimate use of power. Presence of a formalized set of provisions to deal with job impairments is a feature of the work place that is not present in the family, the relationship between doctor and patient, or the judicial system. The work place offers a superior opportunity for intervention and the introduction of legitimate social controls" (xv). Perhaps another way of saying this is that to a much greater extent than other kinds of social arrangements the work-site—potentially at least—is characterized by a degree of objectivity that indicates clearly when, how, and why power is to be used. That that degree of objectivity is not always clear, or that power is sometimes not used in appropriate ways or even held in abeyance contrary to what a situation may suggest, indicates a lack of knowledge about the nature and purpose of the worksite or about the nature and purpose of the management function or both.

The worksite-based contractual arrangement between employers and employees is also the reason why one of the most important steps in implementing an employee assistance program is supervisor training (which we will explore shortly in detail), especially the kind of super-visor training that elucidates the nature of the relationship between employers and employees. Donald W. Myers, in his excellent book *Establishing and Building Employee Assistance Programs*, tells us what happens when good intentions are not followed by appropriate action: "Implementing an EAP should begin with a well-planned and executed supervisory training program. One organization hired a counselor, con-structed special counseling facilities, distributed literature publicizing the program to employees, even established a joint union-management EAP advisory committee, and then short-changed the entire effort by restrict-ing supervisory training to a brief orientation that simply explained the program's mechanics" (235). If supervisor training is to be effective, that is, if it is to sufficiently impress upon supervisors the importance of their role in the EAP and the importance of their responsibilities as supervi-sors, then it must go beyond the mere mechanics of the program and focus on the nature of the employer-employee relationship, the impor-tance of early identification of less than satisfactory job performance, and the purpose of constructive confrontation. It must, in short, focus on the *conceptual* structure as well as the practical or mechanical aspects of employee assistance. It is not too much to say—as indeed it was once said—that the supervisor is the key person in the implementation and maintenance of an employee assistance program and that without his knowledge of and participation in the program, it will not be effective. At the risk of some repetition and perhaps sounding somewhat simplistic, it must be emphasized to supervisors that their primary responsibility is the monitoring of job performance and that their use of sanctions to enforce work performance standards in the work place are the usual and essential components of the management process and are intrinsic to that process. As Myers suggests: "Supervisors will exhibit enthusiasm and *initiative* in an EAP if the training phase 1) outlines the supervisor's role in the procedure, 2) describes in detail how supervisors can assume their roles (define performance criteria, communicate expectations to employees, check performance, recognize deficiencies and excellence, and take action), and 3) explains that supervisors will also be evaluated on their performance in assuming their EAP responsibilities" (235).

To say that an EAP should be understood as a management program is not to say that it is not also an employee benefit, in the widest possible sense. It is, rather, to suggest that to view it as only or primarily an employee benefit is to consign it to a marginal role within the organization. Conversely, to view employee assistance as a management program is also to view it as an employee benefit. Thus, while the concept of employee assistance-as-management program easily incorporates the concept of employee benefit, the reverse is not true; employee assistance-as-employee benefit tends strongly to preclude any understanding of employee assistance as an integrated formalized management program and leaves EAPs extremely vulnerable to fashion. For after all is said and done, employee assistance is no more and no less than a conceptualization and systematization of sound management principles and practice.

If we could abstract from the foregoing the basic principles of employee assistance-as-management program model, as we did earlier with the employee assistance-as-employee benefit model, we would come up with the following:

1. employee assistance is a core function of the management process and is integrated into and integral to that process;
2. the emphasis is on job performance, not employee personal problems;
3. there is substantive supervisor training, emphasizing both the conceptual and technical structure of employee assistance, hence greater supervisor involvement; the emphasis is on early identification and constructive confrontation of the troubled employee on the basis of impaired job performance; and
4. there will be increased referrals of people with alcohol and drug problems and increased referrals of those with serious emotional problems.

Several years ago, in the course of doing a supervisor training session for a group of supervisors at a hospital in California, I was asked the following question by one of the supervisors in attendance: "What right do I have to violate the autonomy of my employees?" Her question came on the heels of a discussion about the legitimacy of supervisor intervention in those cases where job performance was less than adequate. Behind that supervisor's question lies a cultural ethos that endorses an extreme form of individualism, but that's a story for another time and another place. More important for our purposes, the supervisor's question also betrayed a great deal of uncertainty or ambiguity about her role and responsibilities as a supervisor. As noted earlier, her concern is neither unique nor unusual; many, perhaps most, supervisors get little or nothing in the way of substantive management training. If they receive any training at all, it is usually technical or formulaic in nature, at one extreme, or, at the other, a kind of feel-good exhortation based supposedly on spiritual principles and presented by a high-priced management guru who, alone in the universe, has recently discovered the "secret" of good management practice. Seldom is there much discussion about the fact that management means, first and foremost, dealing with human beings in their infinite variety and concrete and specific human behaviors. This is not to deny that there may be and frequently are technical aspects to management, nor is it to deny that human beings are more than merely "resources." It is, rather, to suggest that the volitional nature of human behavior must be the primary focus of any kind of management training. And this is where EAP supervisor training comes in. If management is anything at all, it is, as a friend of mine once defined it, "the art of developing relationships," relationships that are based on explicit and mutual expectations, hence on trust.

Of all of the components of an employee assistance program, none is more important than supervisor training. It encapsulates the nature and purpose of employee assistance, connects the supervisor to the EAP, strengthens the management process, enhances opportunities for the troubled employee whose job performance is less than satisfactory to get the help he needs, and contributes to increased productivity.

More precisely perhaps, because it is the foundation of an effective employee assistance program, supervisor training permits the development of a partnership between the EAP and the supervisor, a partnership that underscores the fact that the EAP is not merely a kind of external technical resource for supervisors but is, in fact, an integral part of the organization designed to further the supervisor's, the employee's, and the organization's goals. Herein lies the importance of supervisor training: It enhances and formalizes the process of communication, not only between the supervisor and the employee but between the supervisor, the employee, the organization, and the EAP. Without a well-developed supervisor training program, the employee assistance program will remain remote, detached, and ultimately incapable of participating in the internal dynamics of the organization or contributing to the well-being of employees. For all of these reasons, it is crucially important that supervisors understand employee assistance in a conceptual as well as a technical sense. Myers maintains that: "[s]upervisors are not going to commit themselves to an EAP, particularly since confrontation is involved, unless [they] are *sensitized* to the program's objectives through training that (1) explains the pervasiveness of treatable problems among the workforce, (2) details the problem-work deficiency relationship, (3) describes the costs to the organization attributable to the deficiencies of troubled employees, and (4) explains how the EAP can help the supervisor do a better job by reducing performance deficiencies" (235).

Given the nature of the American workplace today—with its emphasis on increased productivity, mergers and downsizing, and the pernicious notion of "doing more with less"—Myers's words are especially pertinent, for a number of reasons. First, in all too many instances, there is a great deal of ambiguity about the supervisor's responsibilities, his authority, and his relationship to those he supervises and to those who supervise him. If it is the case that employee job descriptions are frequently unclear or nonexistent, it is also the case that supervisor job descriptions are frequently unclear or nonexistent. Second, very few supervisors receive any management training and certainly not the kind of training that would enable them to confront constructively the problem employee. Most supervisors are promoted up through the ranks, without any kind of preparation for their new responsibilities and on the basis of the questionable assumption that because they did a good job at one level they will do the same at another level, which completely ignores the essential differences in job requirements. Third, because of the very nature of the workplace today, many supervisors know only a kind of crisis management. Feeling pressure from the people above them and from the people below them, not at all certain of the legitimacy or extent of their authority, questioning perhaps their own competence, and frequently not certain of the kind of support they will receive from their supervisors, many supervisors, in effect, abdicate their responsibilities and focus almost exclusively, as a supervisor confided to me on one occasion, on "keeping the lid on," that is, preventing or circumscribing crisis situations. And finally, for a variety of reasons, very few supervisors understand management as the art of developing relationships. Instead, they understand management solely in terms of the accomplishment of specific and concrete tasks and the people they supervise as means to those ends. In view of the fact that very few supervisors receive any kind of substantive management training, this is not surprising.

Before we pursue the topic of supervisor training in greater detail, it might be well to review the Core Technology of employee assistance, for two reasons: (1) the Core Technology defines the essential principles of employee assistance, which in turn shape the unique relationship between employee assistance and the worksite; and (2) it is what distinguishes employee assistance from other efforts within the broad range of the human services. First formulated by Terry Blum and Paul Roman in the March 1985 issue of *The Almacan*, and later adopted by EAPA in revised form, these principles describe the nature and purpose of employee assistance. First, the Core Technology as outlined by Blum and Roman (16–17, all italics are in the original):

1. *Identification of employees' behavior problems based on job performance issues.*

2. *Provision of expert consultation to supervisors, managers, and union stewards on how to take the appropriate steps in utilizing employee assistance policy and procedures.*

3. *Availability and appropriate use of constructive confrontation.*

4. *Micro-linkages with counseling, treatment and other community resources.*

5. *The creation and maintenance of macro-linkages between the work organization and counseling, treatment and other community resources.*

6. *The centrality of employees' alcohol problems as the program focus with the most significant promise for producing recovery and genuine cost savings for the organization in terms of future performance and reduced benefit usage.*

Now the Core Technology as outlined in the 1999 edition of the *EAPA Standards and Professional Guidelines for Employee Assistance Professionals* (v):

[1] Consultation with, training of, and assistance to work organization leadership [managers, supervisors, and union stewards] seeking to manage the troubled employee, enhance the work environment, and improve employee job performance; and, outreach to and education of employees and their family members about availability of EAP services;

[2] Confidential and timely problem identification/assessment services for employee clients with personal concerns that may affect job performance;

[3] Use of constructive confrontation, motivation, and short-term intervention with employee clients to address problems that affect job performance;

[4] Referral of employee clients for diagnosis, treatment, and assistance, plus case monitoring and follow-up services;

[5] Consultation to work organization in establishing and maintaining effective relations with treatment and other service providers, and in managing provider contracts;

[6] Consultation to work organization to encourage availability of and employee access to health benefits covering medical and behavioral problems, including, but not limited to, alcoholism, drug abuse, and mental and emotional disorders; and

[7] Identification of the effects of EAP services on the work organization and individual job performance.

Although the Core Technology as adopted by EAPA is the "official" version, it is substantively weaker because less specific than Blum and Roman's, for two reasons. First, as we noted in Chapter 3, the diminished status and significance of alcohol problems in the workplace in EAPA's version changes considerably the focus and context of employee assistance, in effect attenuating its relationship to the worksite. Second, EAPA's version of the Core Technology is less specific than Blum and Roman's version in one important respect: Although EAPA's version mentions constructive confrontation, it is not explicit in what is perhaps the single most important aspect of employee assistance, that is, the identification of the troubled employee on the basis of impaired job performance. This may appear to some as no more than a kind of nitpicking, and the objection may be that the notion of identifying the troubled employee on the basis of impaired job performance is obvious, or that it goes without saying, or that it is implicit in or encapsulated by the first and third items in EAPA's version of the Core Technology, but given its importance to the effectiveness of employee assistance, it should be made clear beyond any doubt, as it is in item one in Blum and Roman's version, that this is the basis, the very heart of employee assistance. Indeed, to a very great degree, employee assistance stands or falls on this simple premise.

With these important qualifications in mind, we may say that the Core Technology contains the principles that define the profession and provide the conceptual framework for integrating employee assistance into the organizational structure. Absent these principles, an employee assistance program will not be effective simply because it will not, and cannot, be an integral or essential part of the organization. Absent these principles, there will be little or no consultation or communication between supervisors and consultants, hence little or no comprehension on the part of supervisors about the nature and purpose of employee assistance, little or no understanding on the part of employees about the nature and purpose of employee assistance or about the availability of services, and, finally, little or no support by executive management for the program. And since it is those in executive management who ultimately will provide or withhold their imprimatur for the program, the absence of these principles will almost certainly insure its failure. In fact, absent these principles, there is no such thing as employee assistance.

It is also important to note that the Core Technology is not a hypothesis or a theory; it is a conceptual framework containing several principles that are derived from the actual practice of EAPs. Its foci, or principles, are several: the troubled employee, especially the troubled employee whose job performance is impaired; management, and the crucial role played by management in implementing and maintaining EAPs and in identifying the troubled employee on the basis of impaired job performance; and constructive confrontation, without which the notion of an employee assistance program makes very little sense. These, in turn, suggest the ends for which EAPs are implemented: the resolution of problem situations in the workplace, increased productivity, and organizational development. All else, including assessment and referral, case management, and providers and provider contracts or "linkages," is secondary, that is, they are means and not ends. What has happened with many EAPs, unfortunately, is that means and ends have been reversed or, more precisely, what used to be the ends have been discarded in favor of counseling programs of one kind or another.

Writing in the March/April 1998 issue of the *Exchange*, Dan Feerst and Dodie Gill outline "six reasons why the core technology (CT) is vital to the profession" (16–17):

(1) The CT uniquely defines the EA field and clearly separates it from the functions of other human service professions.

(2) The CT inhibits the creation of programs and services with missing parts that mistakenly call themselves EAPs (an EAP does not exist without the core technology).

(3) The CT allows for the critical education of business executives and owners and other EAP consumers, who need to be made aware of what constitutes a functional EAP.

(4) The CT enhances the ability of EAPA chapters to push more successfully for state licensure.

(5) The CT defines specific core functions.

(6) The CT is a common denominator for facilitating communication among EA professionals.

Although all six of the elements outlined by Feerst and Gill are important for understanding the Core Technology as that which defines employee assistance as a profession and as a practical endeavor, it is the first and fifth that anchor employee assistance and clearly distinguish it from other efforts within the human services. And it is this—the Core Technology as that which clearly defines the field and specifies its core functions— that is noticeably absent in many programs that call themselves EAPs. In other words, it is the Core Technology that states explicitly what employee assistance is and what it is not.

In the end, however, the importance granted to or withheld from the Core Technology is determined by communication. The more frequent the communication about employee assistance, the more likely it is that both employees and supervisors will use the program. But the reverse is also true; where communication is absent or sporadic, the less likely it is that the program will be used. Writing in the July 1994 issue of *Employee Assistance*, Paul Roman laments "the extent to which communication and education about the EA system is neglected as a priority because EA workers busy themselves with the interactions required by their multiple roles." He stresses the importance of communication "to the success of the continuing impact of EA activity in a specific workplace" (11). The evidence suggests, Roman believes, that there is a direct correlation between employee knowledge of the employee assistance program and the degree to which employees and family members use it. Thus, in all of its forms, communication about the employee assistance program is essential for all employees in the organization, for those whose job performance is adequate as well as for those whose performance is inadequate and for those who supervise the latter. Such communication is vital if the EAP is to have a taken-for-granted quality among employees and if it is to remain an essential part of the supervisor's daily planning and activities. As Roman also suggests in the same essay: "EA service use can take on a whole new flavor if the entire workplace is made aware of why the EA effort is in place. Keeping a lid on these motives would be foolish because they are almost always reflective of a fairly decent regard for the well-being of the workforce" (12).

As important as communication and education are, they are frequently neglected, and this is especially true for one of the most important, if not the most important, components of employee assistance—supervisor training. I know from my own experience with EAPs, both here in Wichita and elsewhere in the country, that many EAP practitioners will go to great lengths to provide general information about their services—brochures, posters, monthly or quarterly newsletters, and so forth—but are reluctant to emphasize the importance of supervisor training to their organizational clients. This may reflect the fact, as Roman suggests, that employee assistance practitioners are involved in all sorts of multiple and miscellaneous activities, and supervisor training is demanding and time consuming. But it may also reflect the fact that there is a great deal of ignorance on the part of these same practitioners about supervisor training and its importance, or the fact that their corporate clients are not amenable to granting the time necessary for such training. However much these factors play a part, one thing is certain: The lack of supervisor training is a consequence of the diminished role of management in the eyes of some EAP practitioners.

If the problem is ignorance on the part of employee assistance practitioners about the purpose and importance of supervisor training, it might be well if these EAPs were not implemented at all. If it is the case that executive management is not willing to permit supervisor training because it is time consuming, it would suggest that employee assistance is not well understood by these managers, which in turn would suggest that the initial implementation of the program was faulty. In any case, the lack of supervisor training almost certainly guarantees the failure of the program. In that same article on communication in the July 1994 issue of *Employee Assistance*, Paul Roman makes some extremely pertinent comments on the importance of supervisor training to an effective employee assistance program. Stating that "it is genuinely alarming to learn how little effort is devoted to supervisor training" (11), Roman makes the case for the importance of supervisor training: "Supervisor training takes a good deal of time, resources, and coordination. But its value cannot be overestimated. Such training should be viewed as the training of additional EA staff. Indeed, as key actors in diffusing and implementing EA principles, supervisors become informal members of the EA staff." Roman's words, especially those pertaining to supervisors as informal members of the EA staff, remind us once again of the importance of integrating the EAP as thoroughly as possible into the structure of the organization and the importance of understanding the role of management as pivotal to the effective functioning of an employee assistance program. In the end, these two are the same.

Moreover, there are serious consequences to slighting or ignoring supervisor training, not the least of which is the dissemination of a great deal of misinformation about employee assistance. Roman makes this point also: "The absence of training does not simply mean the absence of knowledge. It more likely means the haphazard diffusion of incomplete, incorrect, or inappropriate knowledge." The absence of supervisor training means, in effect, the absence of employee assistance, for at least two reasons: absent supervisor training, supervisors will have no knowledge of either of its two most important principles—identification of the troubled employee on the basis of impaired job performance *and* constructive confrontation; and second, the policy statement, if there is one, will be utterly meaningless if supervisors do not know how to implement it.

Thus, the only way one can view supervisor training is to see it as the heart or the essence of the Core Technology and the latter, in turn, as the heart or essence of employee assistance. Remove supervisor training from the Core Technology and not only the Core Technology but the whole conceptual framework of employee assistance vanishes. Perhaps another way of saying this is that the absence of supervisor training does not mean merely the absence of one component of employee assistance but the absence of employee assistance. Unlike other aspects of the Core Technology—for example, employee orientation to the EAP, however this may be done—which are necessary but not sufficient conditions for an effectively functioning EAP, supervisor training is both a necessary and the sufficient condition of employee assistance. Nor is supervisor training something that can be done once and then forgotten; there is always employee turnover, which suggests the necessity of doing supervisor training (and employee orientation) on a regular or periodic basis. And even in those cases where supervisors have been trained in the principles and practice of employee assistance, refresher training is important, for as Paul Roman suggests, "even though considerable cost may go into training and education, people forget. It is critical for EA members to think in terms of refresher training for supervisors and refresher education for the general employee population." There is also another benefit to training that, Roman believes, "can be substantially more than reinforcement." "Workplace issues and EA roles related to those issues change with great rapidity. Training and education provide critical opportunities for important updating, as well as assuring an EA image of vitality and responsiveness to changes in the internal and external organizational environments."

What all of this suggests is that supervisor training entails more than merely a kind of nuts-and-bolts rundown on the technical features of an employee assistance program. An EAP, if it is not merely to be a policy on paper, a "court of last resort," or a passive entity existing somewhere on the fringes of the organization (which is the case with a great many EAPs today), must take an active role in making its presence felt. Training, then, should be educative in the best sense of that word since it is essential (1) to integrating the principles and practice of employee assistance into the management structure of the organization, and (2) in making those principles and practice a normal or taken-for-granted part of the education of supervisors in sound management practice. To put this another way, and perhaps broaden the context, it is to suggest that the worksite, normally thought of as compartmentalized, both actually and conceptually, and as having little or nothing to do with the employee's personal life, becomes a kind of support system for the employee. The line between the employee's personal life and work life becomes less than distinct, and the worksite, because it brings together the employee, the employer, and the EAP, and because it incorporates many of the dynamics of human interaction, becomes the common ground where productivity, in its broadest sense, and personal well-being, the former actually a function of the latter, come together. Thus supervisor training, if it is grounded in a philosophy of management that actually, that is, practically, concretely, and actively, rather than merely passively or abstractly, emphasizes the fundamental importance of the individual person to the well-being of the organization, can contribute to creating an organizational structure that is supportive of the best efforts of both employers and employees.

What, then, is supervisor training, and what does it entail? How does it enhance supervisory skills and, by extension, contribute to the well-being of the organization and its people? First, it is important to note that EAP supervisor training is management training and not merely an add-on to existing organizational management training programs (if there are such) or an afterthought. For obvious reasons, the notion that EAP supervisor training is somehow or in some way outside of mainstream management practice is lethal to the effective functioning of any EAP. Here again, assessing management commitment to the program is crucial. Farmer and Maynard are instructive in this regard: "[A]ny supervisory or management training must be integrated into regular company training practices. If all management training is done by a training department except that EAP-related training is done by the EAP coordinator, the company is clearly communicating that appropriate use of the EAP is not really part of mainstream management expectations. To integrate the program fully requires that the EAP coordinator work with the regular trainers to have EAP principles incorporated at all relevant points into their courses" (34). Once more we encounter the word "integrate" and once again we are reminded of the overriding importance of integrating every facet of employee assistance into the structure and daily routines and activities of the organization.

Second, supervisors must understand supervisor training and employee assistance from a conceptual as well as a technical perspective. In their *Strategies for Employee Assistance Programs: The Crucial Balance*, William J. Sonnenstuhl and Harrison M. Trice provide the conceptual model for supervisor training: "Generally, the model consists of (1) defining program policy, (2) emphasizing the degree of management support for it, (3) explaining the supervisors' role in implementing it, and (4) demonstrating how it can be integrated into supervisors' existing responsibilities for employee job performance" (16). Although all four of the elements of the model outlined by Sonnenstuhl and Trice are essential to the effective training of supervisors and, by extension, essential to the effective functioning of employee assistance programs, it is the first item—"defining program policy"—that is central; unless supervisors understand the nature and purpose of employee assistance, the remaining three elements of the model may not be understood, at least not as well as they should be. The policy itself is the foundation for all that follows, including management support for the EAP, the implementation of the program, and its acceptance by supervisors as a legitimate and necessary part of their responsibilities.

The second element of the model—"emphasizing the degree of management support" for the program—is also essential in that it is derived from the principles contained in the policy statement (again, a major reason for initiating the implementation of an EAP with a well-written and comprehensive policy statement) and is made actual and concrete through the provision of supervisor training. Many, perhaps most, of those employee assistance programs that fail do so because management, especially executive management, is not wholly committed to the program, or, what is the same thing, view the program as no more than an employee benefit, nice to have or useful in some extra-organizational way but not essential to organizational development. The program then languishes on the periphery of the institution, essentially useless. But there is also another reason for emphasizing the importance of management support for the program, and that is that supervisors at all levels tend to take their cues from the level of supervision above them. If supervisors know or sense that their supervisors are lukewarm about the program, or see it, as mentioned above, as merely an employee benefit and as having little or nothing to do with their responsibilities or with organizational development, then they too will assign it the same degree of importance. (One of the most successful EAPs I've ever been associated with was that of a large corporation in which the top executive in the company took part in all of the supervisor training sessions. Although he could not be present for every session, he provided us with a five-minute videotape in which he made clear to every supervisor in the company that the EAP was an integral part of the management structure of the company and that its principles would be incorporated into every management training session. He also made clear that he expected every supervisor to use the program when working with a troubled employee whose job performance was less than satisfactory.)

The third element in the model—"explaining the supervisors' role in implementing" the program—is no less essential than the second element. The crucial point here is that supervisors understand that the principles and practice of employee assistance *are* the principles and practice of sound management practice. This element of the model takes on added significance when the training is done with supervisors who have had little or no management training or, at the opposite pole, with supervisors who have been exposed to abstract or purely technical or formulaic kinds of management training. In the first instance, those supervisors who have had very little management training may feel overwhelmed when initially presented with the program and at the same time told that they will be evaluated, partially at least, on how well and to what degree they have used the program to manage troubled employees. Here it is of the utmost importance that the person doing the training emphasize, over and over again if necessary, that the supervisor's efforts will have the full support of the EAP, and that, in fact, the relationship between the supervisor and the EAP is that of a partnership directed towards the same positive goal, that of returning the troubled employee to full productivity. The supervisor must know and understand that he can contact the EAP at any time and that the latter is always available to walk him through the steps necessary to achieve that goal. Here again we see the importance of integrating the program into the organizational structure. In the second instance, that of supervisors who have had management training of the kind mentioned above, the tendency may be either to view EAP supervisor training as no more than another unnecessary burden added on to what is already a stressful situation, or to see it as an inferior kind of training and therefore of little value (I never cease to be surprised by our culture's penchant for approaching every issue, situation, circumstance, or problem from a purely technical point of view). In these cases, the trainer must emphasize the very practical aspects and advantages of the program, including, but not limited to, the support available from the

EAP, the fact that the program is designed to lighten the supervisor's burden by relieving him of the responsibility to solve the troubled employee's personal problem (this is another area in which I never cease to be surprised by how often supervisors believe that it is their responsibility to solve employees' personal problems), and the fact that he, the supervisor, has the support of his supervisor. If supervisor training achieves anything at all, it should be that of getting across to supervisors the immense practicality of the program. Moreover, EAP supervisor training has one great advantage over most other kinds of management training, and that is that the EAP is a permanent fixture, integrated into the structure of the organization and therefore always available, unlike those types of training programs that are done by outside consultants who, once they complete their assignment, move on to the next company, usually never to be seen again.

The last element of the model—"demonstrating how it can be integrated into supervisors' existing responsibilities for employee job performance"—is also essential, for one reason if for no other: It makes clear that EAP supervisor training *is* management training and not something that is merely adjunctive to whatever other responsibilities the supervisor may have. Indeed, it speaks directly to the fact that the supervisor's primary responsibility is the monitoring of employee job performance and that the training is designed to enhance those skills that will make him more effective as a supervisor. This is a theme that must be stressed over and over again. All too often EAP practitioners tend to slight this aspect of supervisor training either because they are unsure of their ability to do the training or, worse yet, harbor doubts about the legitimacy of supervisor training and, by implication, employee assistance. These, it must be said, are two of the major reasons why employee assistance programs are not effective and why they are vulnerable to fads and trends that are inimical to their effectiveness. It would be well if these programs were never implemented.

Integrating the employee assistance program into the management structure of an organization is a technical as well as a conceptual process. Most supervisor training programs follow a four- or five-step process that, although it may vary somewhat from company to company, includes information on how to identify early on instances of declining or inadequate job performance, how to document poor performance as well as superior performance, how to confront the employee in a constructive manner, how to refer the employee to the EAP, and how to work with that employee after he has been referred to the EAP. In an excellent pamphlet entitled *What an Executive Should Know About Employee As-*

sistance Programs, Gary Fair outlines the advantages to be had when supervisors follow this procedure: "This procedure does much for the supervisors and the company. It frees them up from having to personally deal with employee problems. It allows them to turn the matter over to more qualified professionals and return their attention to their own job. Regardless of the fact that whether a company has an EAP or not, a supervisor has to deal with a subordinate who isn't performing up to standard. The major difference is that, with an EAP, the supervisor has professional outside assistance and an alternative to discipline" (21–22).

Fair's summary of the process points up the advantages to the supervisor of an employee assistance program that has a strong supervisor training component. First, it delineates clearly and succinctly those responsibilities that are the supervisor's and those that are the EAP's, a delineation that is clearly desirable if the supervisor and the program are to be effective. It has been said repeatedly but needs to be said again and again that the supervisor is the key figure in the implementation and maintenance of an employee assistance program, and to the degree that he incorporates the principles and practice of employee assistance into his normal daily activities, to that degree both he and the program will be successful. Second, it provides the supervisor with a positive alternative to what would be the only two negative alternatives open to him in the absence of the program: to continue to tolerate substandard job performance or to take disciplinary action that could lead quickly and easily to serious job action, including suspension or even termination. Third, the training provides the supervisor with a conceptual framework for understanding how the employee assistance program can help to make his job easier and his efforts more effective. And, finally, it provides the supervisor with practical skills that enable him to take prudent and objective measures in cases of inadequate job performance. This last leads us into what is probably the most important part of supervisor training and that which is probably of the greatest concern to supervisors—confronting an employee about impaired or poor job performance, or, what is known in the employee assistance field as constructive confrontation.

The strategy of constructive confrontation is designed to help the troubled employee whose job performance is inadequate or declining return to full productivity. Sonnenstuhl and Trice tell us that the structure of constructive confrontation "is based on both academic and applied research and basic industrial relations practices that suggest that most people can be motivated to change if they receive appropriate feedback about their behavior." They describe the idea of constructive confrontation this way: "For constructive confrontation to be effective, a supervisor may need to hold a number of discussions with an employee whose performance is unacceptable. In the confrontational part of the initial discussion, the employee is given the specifics of unacceptable work performance and warned that continued unacceptable performance is likely to lead to formal discipline. In the constructive part, supervisors remind employees that practical assistance is available through the EAP. Subsequent steps in the process depend on the response of the employee. If performance improves, nothing happens; if unacceptable performance continues, several more informal discussions follow" (25). It is important to note that the strategy of constructive confrontation is designed to retain the troubled employee, if possible. And for this reason, unlike the more traditional approach, which was confrontational only and essentially punitive, constructive confrontation is a kind of dual track approach, if you will, a "carrot and stick approach," which at one and the same time cautions the employee that unacceptable job performance will not continue to be tolerated—formal discipline is always waiting in the wings— and that if he wishes he can receive help through the EAP. Thus the strategy of constructive confrontation accomplishes three important ends: (1) it informs the employee that the company hopes to continue to employ him because it values his skills, which in and of itself is an incentive for the employee to seek help; (2) he is informed, if he did not already know, of precisely what his job deficiencies are and how they are to be corrected; and (3) he knows that assistance is available and that the company will help to provide that assistance if he wishes. This last is especially important if the employee is experiencing alcohol and/or drug problems or a serious emotional problem. It's not likely that an employee will be able to resolve these kinds of problems by himself.

It is also important to note that in the process of constructive confrontation, if it is to be effective, the supervisor must provide the employee with specific instances of unacceptable job performance. It is not enough for the supervisor to generalize about the employee's performance problems, for this may leave the employee confused about exactly what his performance deficiencies are and create a situation in which the supervisor and the employee are talking past one another. This brings us to what is one of the most important aspects of constructive confrontation—documentation.

For the strategy of constructive confrontation to be effective, it is important that the supervisor have written documentation that details the employee's job performance deficiencies. The documentation does not have to be voluminous, but it should be specific regarding incidents, dates, times, and places. Indeed, the more specific the better. Good documentation is important for two reasons: (1) in the event there is any question about the employee's performance or the supervisor's response to it, good documentation can reduce both uncertainty and ambiguity, hence the possibility of misunderstanding and even the possibility of legal problems; and (2) when and if the supervisor needs to confront an employee about his performance, good documentation provides an indispensable structure for the conversation. Because the supervisor needs to keep the focus on job performance issues, and not permit himself to be distracted by personal issues or problems, good documentation provides him with a means of keeping the conversation focused on the performance deficiencies in question and what needs to be done to correct them. Good documentation is a necessary prelude to successful confrontation and can go a long way towards reducing the supervisor's anxiety about confronting the troubled employee. The objective, after all, is to help the employee improve his job performance, thereby enabling the company to retain a valued and valuable employee. The absence of good documentation is the major reason why constructive confrontation so often fails. It is important to note also that good documentation will include instances of satisfactory and even superior performance, if such there are, and usually there are; one of the goals of the supervisor in the strategy of constructive confrontation is not only the effort to retain the employee, if possible, but to inform him that his performance in the past has been satisfactory and that he, the supervisor, is willing to help him improve his performance. In short, the emphasis in constructive confrontation should be on the word "constructive."

If informal discussions with the employee do not produce the desired results, the next step in the strategy of constructive confrontation is introduced. Sonnenstuhl and Trice describe it this way: "Eventually, if the employee's performance still does not improve, a supplementary tactic called *crisis precipitation* is added. At this stage the employee is formally disciplined for continued poor performance—initially with a written warning, then with a series of increasingly long temporary suspensions, and finally with discharge. At all times up until discharge, however, the employee is free to choose to go to the EAP for help" (26). What we have here is a process that starts with informal discussions and, if necessary, proceeds to formal disciplinary action, all the while offering the employee help through the employee assistance program. And herein lies precisely one of the major advantages of a well-implemented employee assistance program with a strong supervisor training component: When supervisors are knowledgeable about the principles and practice of employee assistance, have been trained in the strategy of constructive confrontation, and know that their supervisors and executive management are strongly committed to the program, they are much more likely to use it and intervene early on rather than wait until the situation reaches crisis proportions. The importance of early intervention when a clear pattern of job impairment becomes obvious cannot be overestimated and is a crucial cornerstone of employee assistance programming. I've seen it happen all too often in those cases where supervisor training has not been emphasized or where it is mentioned only in passing that the supervisor is reluctant to act when he should and responds only when the situation escalates into a crisis of some magnitude, or, just as frequently, responds with anger and acts arbitrarily. Another way of looking at this, and this is merely a variation on the preceding point, is that a well-implemented EAP and supervisors trained in the strategy of constructive confrontation provide the entire process with not only objective guidelines at each step in the process but also with safeguards that guarantee a fair hearing for the employee, if you will, a kind of workplace due process.

Although the steps in the formal disciplinary process may vary from company to company, depending on the company's policies and procedures, this is, generally, the process to be followed in the strategy of constructive confrontation. It has been my experience that when there is good documentation and prudent application of the principle of constructive confrontation, the great majority of employees who are experiencing job performance problems will improve their performance.

All of this is but another way of saying that the absence of supervisor training does not mean merely the absence of a particular component of employee assistance—it means, rather, the absence of employee assistance. This is so for several reasons. First, supervisor training is not merely a component of employee assistance; it is employee assistance. Absent supervisor training, especially its focus on the management process generally and the indispensable role of management in insuring the effectiveness of that process, there is no employee assistance program. It makes no sense to speak of employee assistance as a worksite-based management program or even a worksite-based program and at the same time deny or minimize the importance of supervisor training. Brochures, newsletters, posters, and employee orientations, as important as they are, are not substitutes for supervisor training. Second, and this is a corollary of the first point, when supervisor training is missing, knowledge of the entire conceptual structure of employee assistance is denied to supervisors, including executive management. The fact that supervisor training *is* management training, the fact that employee assistance can perform a valuable consultative function for both supervisors and employees, and the fact that the EAP is an integral part of the institution and not merely a loosely attached appendage, are all essential aspects of the implementation, development, and maintenance of employee assistance programs. Absent supervisor training, supervisors will have at best only sketchy knowledge of the program and probably a great deal of misinformation. Third, absent supervisor training, supervisors will have little or no knowledge of the concept and practice of constructive confrontation—the principle that is or should be central to management practice. Constructive confrontation involves more than merely confronting the troubled employee about substandard job performance; it involves also, and most importantly, a mentoring function in that it describes and explicates standards, provides for an objective evaluation process, and offers the employee the support necessary to improve job performance. Finally, supervisor training provides the supervisor with the knowledge that the EAP is there to support his efforts as well as those of his subordinates. It also offers the supervisor the opportunity for self-evaluation and suggests to him the essential nature of sound management practice and the integral nature of management precept and practice.

Thus supervisor training is a great deal more than a method or procedure for confronting employees about performance problems; its importance lies in the fact that it speaks directly to supervisors about the essential principles of good management, provides a well-defined context for evaluating performance, including the supervisor's, and performs the function of integrating the EAP into the overall management structure of the institution. Given the importance of supervisor training, it strains credulity to suggest that there can be employee assistance without supervisor training.

At this point we've come full circle: The concept of employee assistance as a worksite-based management program, the integral and integrating nature of supervisor training, and the overarching conceptual and practical nature of the Core Technology, are all aspects of the same foundational process, that of integrating the employee assistance program into organizational processes and procedures. Conversely, the absence of management from employee assistance calls into question not only the very legitimacy of supervisor training but the whole of the Core Technology, for these have only, and no more than, the significance attributed to them by management.

Ideally, the employee assistance program should be just as much a part of the cultural ethos of the organization as production and planning schedules. It should be understood by supervisors as not only a means for identifying the troubled employee based on job performance issues but also as providing objective criteria for performance evaluation and a general philosophy of management. At this point, it might be well, once again, to broaden our context and place the person, whether employee or employer, in a perspective that sees him as more than merely a client or worker. In so doing, we may perhaps get a glimpse of what, ultimately, employee assistance is all about. In his book *The Spirit of Democratic Capitalism*, Michael Novak has some interesting comments on the nature of human nature and what he describes as "virtuous self-interest": "The real interests of individuals . . . are seldom merely self-regarding. To most persons, their families mean more than their own interests; they frequently subordinate the latter to the former. Their communities are also important to them. In the human breast, commitments to benevolence, fellow-feeling, and sympathy are strong. Moreover, humans have the capacity to see themselves as others see them, and to hold themselves to standards that transcend their own selfish inclinations. Thus the 'self' in self-interest is complex, at once familial and communitarian as well as individual, other-regarding as well as self-regarding, cooperative as well as independent, and self-judging as well as self-loving. Understood too narrowly, self-interest destroys firms as surely as it destroys personal lives. Understood broadly enough, as a set of realistic limits, it is the key to all the virtues, as prudence is" (93).

Implicit in Novak's statements, as it is in von Mises and Hazlitt's statements, is the idea that it is persons, endowed with the faculty of reason, and not capital, raw materials, or technology, who decide the fate of a company or an economy or, for that matter, any institution. Extending this idea a bit further and applying it to our subject matter, we may say that since it is persons, not clients or individuals, who are the source of whatever well-being they and societies may have, then the proper role of an employee assistance program is to contribute to creating an environment in which "virtuous self-interest" can come to the fore. If this is a bit too idealistic for some, we might then consider the same thing said in a somewhat more technical way. Again, Charles Weaver: "The notion of a systems approach to training and education is important because of the interlocking nature of our social structures presented by individuals, the company, families, and treatment resources. EAPs make the most sense when they are mainstreamed into the daily functions of the individual and his world. Any approach to personal interventions must consider the entire system affecting the individual" (337). And this is where the employee assistance program can make a singular contribution: If the EAP is part of the management process, if consultation with management, including and especially executive management, on a frequent and regular basis is the norm, and if case management is an integral part of the process, then the employee assistance program will be successful in helping to create an environment that is receptive to personal well-being.

Integrating the employee assistance program into the overall organizational structure is, however, normally a slow process, for several reasons. There is, first, the normal human resistance to change, especially the kind of change that entails the addition or alteration of responsibilities, which in turn may diminish one's sense of control. Supervisors, especially those who have had little or no formal management training, may be resistant to any kind of training that involves changes in their normal routine and that involves, also, the articulation of objective criteria as part of the evaluative process and that, therefore, places the supervisor in a position where he is also evaluated. It is also the case with many supervisors, especially those who have had a kind of management training that is abstract in nature—for example, management by objectives in which a great deal of time and effort is spent distinguishing goals from objectives, or the kind of training that at great lengths attempts to determine the "soul" of the organization, or that is no more than a kind of "pep talk" by a management guru—that something as practical, concrete, and specific as EAP supervisor training may be seen as an inferior species of training. Finally, there are those institutional environments where, because the quest for efficiency is an obsession and micromanagement is compulsive—the two go hand in hand—there is little understanding by management at any level that it is people and not techniques, processes, or procedures that ground the organization. Even so, in many cases, activities such as supervisor training, employee orientation to the EAP, consultation with supervisors about particular employees or specific situations, consultation with executive management and participation in discussions and decisions affecting policies, procedures, goals, and strategies, and responding to conflicts within departments and between and among employees are just a few of the ways in which employee assistance programs can establish that taken-for-granted quality, which is indispensable to effective programs. Other activities, such as frequent assessment of and consultation with client companies to determine their particular needs and problems, providing presentations on various topics, working closely with an advisory board, convening sessions with representatives of client companies for the purpose of seeking advice and assistance on various issues, and periodically providing employees and employers with literature on the employee assistance program are all ways of integrating employee assistance into the worksite. In other words, the implementation, development, and maintenance of an employee assistance program takes a great deal of time, thought, and effort.

When thinking about employee assistance generally and supervisor training particularly, I often recall my friend's definition of management, mentioned above, as "the art of developing relationships." It is precisely and fundamentally that, to a much greater degree than it is a technical process. Indeed, unless management is understood as the art of developing relationships and an employee assistance program as a way of coordinating, supporting, and encouraging those relationships, the program will not be effective. It is the human factor, not the technical factor, that is decisive. Weaver has some interesting things to say about the human relations aspect of supervisor training and, by implication, the worksite-bound nature of employee assistance. "*Human relations training for supervisors* is another integral concept in the program development models. Supervisors are key members of the problem identification and referral process. Vital to their facilitating worker problem resolution is their ability to listen to troubled employees with a nonjudgmental attitude, convey a sense of compassionate understanding, and, yet, remain sufficiently detached to firmly confront them with job performance inadequacies. These are skills for which many supervisors need training beyond what an organization normally provides. However, skills in human relations are vital to motivating workers to seek assistance rather than avoiding their problems and suffering serious consequences" (324).

There are several important ideas expressed here, not the least of which is the idea that "[s]upervisors are key members of the problem identification and referral process," an idea that is, or should be, fundamental or axiomatic to employee assistance. For it is not the employee assistance consultant but the supervisor who has daily and firsthand knowledge of the people he supervises and is therefore in the best position to identify and provide direction for the troubled employee. The process begins and ends with the supervisor and to minimize or ignore his role in identifying, confronting, and referring the employee is to insure the failure of the EAP before it even gets off the ground. Another key idea is conveyed in Weaver's words when he speaks of "a sense of compassionate understanding," which can also be considered fundamental or axiomatic since the way in which the supervisor approaches the troubled employee may well determine the outcome of the entire process. Whatever the job performance problems may be, it is crucial that the supervisor provide a context in which the employee can retain his dignity and self-respect and know that the supervisor's purpose is to help rather than punish. This brings us to our last point, which is really a corollary of the preceding two.

When Weaver states that "skills in human relations are vital to motivating workers to seek assistance rather than avoiding their problems and suffering serious consequences," he is describing what is perhaps the essence of supervision and the single most difficult aspect of the supervisor's job—motivating other people to work together to achieve common and agreed-upon ends. When all is said and done, this is the supervisor's ultimate responsibility, and the employee assistance professional who does not understand this will be of little or no use to employers and employees.

Part III

OF CENTAURS AND SUPERMEN

Chapter 6

EMPLOYEE ASSISTANCE AND MANAGED MENTAL HEALTH CARE

Abstraction is the bane of our age, and nowhere is this more apparent than in our use and abuse of the word "change." In countless books and magazines, in the electronic media, and in newspapers, one never ceases to hear about the glories and wonders of change. Never mind that very few of the people singing paeans of praise to change even bother to tell us what they mean by the word or attempt to describe it empirically in particular events or circumstances. As I suggested in Chapter 1, the word itself has taken on an almost mystical or religious aura, above and beyond criticism and suggesting the possession of magical or transformative qualities. The assumption is that change, despite the rantings of a few reactionaries, is always a positive good.

And, indeed, in many instances, change is beneficial. Whether we are talking about change in the sciences or, broadly, technology, especially information technology, change has been beneficial. Who but a few Luddites would want to turn the clock back in, say, the area of medical technology?

But the notion of change, however we may attempt to define or describe it, is only part of the problem. Of greater concern is the concept of "progress," and the notion, peculiar to moderns, that change always means progress, not only in science and technology, but in other areas of human endeavor as well. The marriage of change and progress is the conceit of our age and one that is reluctant to subject itself to scrutiny.

But scrutinize it we must, for change can just as easily mean regression as well as progression.

In an incisive and insightful essay entitled "Jungians and Gnostics" in the October 1994 issue of *First Things*, Jeffrey Burke Satinover takes a penetrating look at the idea of progress. "As it is with individuals," he suggests, "so it is with cultures, and our own great cultural shibboleth— with us since the Renaissance—is the myth of progress," which "fosters [the] illusion that we are so different from nay, better than—our ances- tors" (41–42). To those who would question Satinover's description of progress as "our own great cultural shibboleth" and maintain that we have made progress, he replies that "[o]f course, in many respects pro- gress has been and is being made. But if we examine ourselves carefully, we will have to agree that the great areas of progress lie in the domain of *technology,* broadly defined." And in perpetuating the myth of an all- encompassing doctrine of progress, we are, Satinover suggests, deluding ourselves. We fail to discriminate between that which is in actual fact progress and which is pure illusion. Satinover describes that illusion this way: "[W]hen we consider our culture as having 'made progress' tacitly we mean far more than mere technological advance. Quite without think- ing, we presume progress in other dimensions as well: that we have progressed 'as people'; that we are 'better', in some sense, than our forbears; 'healthier' not just in the sense of less subject to, say, bacteria, but having acquired a superior mental hygienics; that our way of under- standing the world—our Weltanschauung—has also progressed; that we are, in fact, in some but dimly sensed way, morally superior to those who came before us. This is, after all, how we justify major changes in mores and social policy, and why so often we refer to these changes in all sincerity—even though they more often than not prove disastrous— as progressive."

When Satinover states that we see ourselves as "morally superior to those who came before us," he is elucidating the basic philosophical premise of our age, for we do in fact believe that past ages were a kind of childhood for the human race and that the present age marks a kind of coming of age. This kind of grandiosity is nowhere more apparent than in some of the social sciences, especially, as mentioned above, in the field of psychology. But a belief in this conception of progress can only be sustained by a kind of moral and intellectual amnesia. Again, Satinover: "While we indeed have progressed in certain limited ways, it is not at all clear that we have progressed in those large ways that really are our main concern. For example, what evidence is there that modern man is morally superior to premodern man? Does not the bloody history of the twentieth century suggest the reverse?"

For Satinover, then, the notion of a blanket kind of progress is a myth, and not only a myth but a dangerous myth, for it precludes any understanding of the nature of human nature, hence any understanding of human finitude and limitation. Moreover, we can maintain the notion of an all-encompassing kind of progress only at a terrible price, that of a profound and pervasive contempt for history. Indeed, a contemptuous dismissal of history or, at the very least, a belief that the past is no more than prologue, is a necessary prerequisite for a belief in the doctrine of an all-embracing progress. And once we dismiss history we imagine we are in possession of a clean slate upon which we can write our prescriptions for utopia. The problem, however, is that when we dismiss history, we also dismiss two indispensable virtues, prudence and humility. As Satinover suggests, "[O]nce we realize that the presumption of progress, at least in certain important areas, is a myth, and how, in fact, mere fashion most often dictates the specifics of our presumptions, we also begin to realize how fickle we really are. And once we begin to acknowledge this disconcerting fact, it becomes apparent that within the span of at most a few generations—and often more rapidly than that—a limited set of ideas is likely to be turned over, repackaged (in whatever constitutes the new idiom), and resold as new thinking."

What does all of this have to do with employee assistance? On the surface, perhaps, very little, but as I hope to show, the notions of change and progress or, more precisely, the notion that change always and everywhere means progress is driving much of what is happening in the field of employee assistance today. The literature in the field and, more broadly, in the entire range of the human services, is larded with references to change, growth, and progress. Never mind that these are rarely defined or described; it is enough that they are mentioned, that they have a kind of "needless to say" quality, and that they can be used as warrants for granting legitimacy to whatever trendy notions come into view.

In two areas, especially, those of managed mental health care and the currently fashionable notion of expanded or super EAPs, the doctrine of change as progress has been hard at work in the form of strenuous efforts to show that the former can be integrated with employee assistance without any adverse effects for employee assistance, and, indeed, to demonstrate that integration will improve employee assistance, and, in the case of the latter, that organizations are demanding that employee assistance assume responsibilities that heretofore have not been considered as within the province of employee assistance, all the while maintaining the Core Technology. Among the "EAP-related services," as they are described by EAPA, are such things as wellness programs, disability management, welfare-to-work programs, and outplacement/retirement programs. The contention is that as the workplace changes and becomes more complex, it becomes incumbent upon employee assistance to change also. And change, for its advocates, always means progress. Typical of these sentiments are remarks by Bradley Googins in the April 1994 issue of *Employee Assistance*: "Perhaps the new growth that springs up from the fires of change within EAPs and their organizations offers new opportunities for prevention and for impacting the organization in ways that we had not previously thought about. It might just be that as some of the older roles or functions for the EA professional drop by the wayside or are vendored out to others within the new healthcare system, new opportunities to deal with the stresses and challenges of the re-engineered organization will spring up" (12).

It's difficult to know where or how to begin making sense of this passage. The theme is change, but with the exception of brief and essentially indirect references to change management and corporate reengineering, there is no indication in this passage or, for that matter, anywhere else in the article of what Googins means by change, nor does he indicate specifically what kinds of changes he has in mind. What does "new growth" mean? What is "the new healthcare system"? And what "older roles or functions" should be dropped or passed off "to others within the new healthcare system"? What does it mean to speak of a "re-engineered organization," and how does the latter affect employee assistance? Generally, the passage endorses change without ever becoming specific, and like so much of the literature in the employee assistance field, Googins's article makes no effort to distinguish between what is essential to employee assistance and what is merely adjunctive or peripheral. Before we speak grandiloquently of change ("the fires of change"), we should know specifically what it is we are desirous of changing *and* why. That Googins himself is aware of this particular problem is indicated by a question he asks in the same article: "Are there any boundaries for the new EAP or are we destined to continuously evolve without any core to guide what we stand for and what we become?" Bracketing for the moment whatever it is that Googins means by "the new EAP," this is indeed the central question for employee assistance.

Perhaps nowhere are the uncertainty and confusion about what constitutes employee assistance more in evidence than in the efforts to "integrate" managed mental health care and employee assistance. The past ten to fifteen years have seen all sorts of assertions and efforts to demonstrate that the two can be integrated without any essentially negative effect on employee assistance and that indeed integration will result in stronger or better or more responsive EAPs. This is the tack taken by Carl Tisone in the June 1994 issue of *Employee Assistance*: "As the market for mental health management services has matured, the larger EAP providers have been drawn (sometimes kicking and screaming) into the managed care field. Clients have demanded it. Likewise, specialty MMHC firms have perceived the need to have an EAP component to compete effectively in the marketplace. Thus, the opportunity was created for the corporate customer to do 'one-stop shopping' for EAP and MMHC. The 'integrated' or 'EAP-driven' managed care program has been largely a product of this development" (16).

These words sum up concisely the problems associated with efforts to integrate managed mental health care and employee assistance and, more specifically, efforts to suggest why and how the two are compatible. This passage, like most of the rest of the article, is made up entirely of assertions that are grounded in nothing more than verbal declarations of the compatibility of employee assistance and managed mental health care. Tisone offers us neither evidence nor logic to support these statements. First of all, to state that a (the?) reason for integrating the two is that "clients have demanded it" is to suggest that client demand is equivalent to compatibility, or that client demand—and that alone—confers legitimacy upon the integrated program. To put this another way, and more to the point perhaps, given the absence of anything more substantive than client demand, that is, given the absence of any standard, principle, or norm for determining the legitimacy of the client's demand or the compatibility of employee assistance and managed mental health care, is there anything that Tisone could not include if clients demanded it? That clients demand something is not a criterion for determining whether the demand is legitimate or accords with the principles or purpose of the thing being demanded. What is it that compels assent or suggests that we acquiesce in a demand? Once we ask this question we can no longer assume that mere assertion is sufficient. Only if we assume that a criterion for evaluating such a demand does not exist, which, in our case, is to suggest that employee assistance is completely malleable and lacking in principles or standards, can we grant the client's demand. This is essentially the Carr-McCann thesis all over again and a salutary reminder of Paul Roman's concern about the entrepreneur. This brings us back to the issue of principles or standards.

Secondly, and wittingly or unwittingly, Tisone puts his finger on the problem when he states that "MMHC firms have perceived the need to have an EAP component to compete effectively in the marketplace." Note that Tisone does not say that adding an EAP component will improve the quality of services provided by the managed mental health care (MMHC) program, or that integrating the two will improve the quality of services provided by the EAP—these, I'm sure, are meant to be inferred. But in the absence of any such statement or qualification, one can only conclude that the "EAP component" is of secondary importance and added merely to provide the MMHC program with a competitive edge. On the face of it, this would seem to be the case, and would suggest, further, that Tisone's primary interest is in marketing a product and not in the intrinsic value of that product. And if this were not enough, the use of the word "component" to describe the relationship between employee assistance and managed mental health care would seem to suggest that employee assistance is no more that a subsystem among other subsystems within a parent system, in this case, managed mental health care. If this is the case, it would hardly be accurate to describe the integrated program as "EAP-driven." All of this seems to be no more than mere salesmanship to facilitate the integration of two essentially dissimilar entities. To see this from another and opposite perspective, one need only turn Tisone's statement around and have it read as follows: "Likewise, EAP firms have perceived the need to have an MMHC component to compete effectively in the marketplace." How would one interpret that statement?

Similarly, others of Tisone's statements betray that same apparent inability to develop concepts or ideas in any but the most abstract fashion. What is one to make of the following statements? "The integrated EAP/MMHC program works because its EAP and managed care objectives are harmonious." Or, "Both facets of the integrated program rest on a philosophical foundation that states the most cost-effective care is that which works! In other words, quality of care is consistent with cost-effectiveness—the most efficacious use of resources" (16). Again we are faced with the same problem: It is difficult to know what Tisone means when, for example, he states that EAP and MMHC objectives are "harmonious," or when he states that "the most cost-effective care is that which works." The latter statement is merely tautological, that is, it uses different words to express the same idea. And who determines "that which works"? Moreover, it is mere assertion, providing neither evidence nor argument for the truth of the proposition. It is also difficult to know where to begin to examine Tisone's statements, because like so much of the writing in the employee assistance field they never get below the level of a kind of global abstraction that simply makes assertions; there is little concreteness or particularity. For example, what is one to make of phrases like "philosophical foundation" and "the most efficacious use of resources," or sentences like "quality of care is consistent with cost-effectiveness"? How or in what way does "the integrated program rest on a philosophical foundation"? What is the philosophical foundation? A tautology is not a philosophical foundation. To repeat, these are merely vague assertions representative of the tone and substance of much of the writing on managed mental health care in the employee assistance field. To take just one more example: How are the objectives of employee assistance and managed mental health care "harmonious"? What does "harmonious" mean, and by what standards, principles, or norms are the objectives of employee assistance and managed mental health care harmonious? The word "harmonious" is frequently no more than a stand-in for clear or logical thinking and lends itself easily to any effort to gather up all sorts of discordant and discrepant elements, burnish and link them in the abstract, and then assert that the abstraction coincides perfectly with reality.

Lest I be accused of taking Tisone's words out of context or of using them merely for the purpose of polemics, I would like to point to an earlier essay by Tisone in the February 1994 issue of the *Exchange*, in which the context is the debate within the employee assistance field about the Core Technology and expanded EAPs. In this essay Tisone states: "There will be programs at both ends of the spectrum which succeed and which fail, due far more to the talent and perseverance of the program managers than on the underlying philosophy regarding program boundaries" (11). In other words, success—whatever that may mean—is the only standard, and an "underlying philosophy regarding program boundaries," that is, principles, is unnecessary. But if an underlying philosophy or principles are unnecessary, then what determines the form and shape of employee assistance? Tisone is not at a loss for an answer: "I believe a trend will emerge that will essentially determine the next phase of EAP evolution. That trend may be modestly affected by our current debate over EAP boundaries, *but it will be primarily driven by marketplace forces.* Indeed, I suspect that we in the EAP field frequently overestimate the value of our 'professional' opinions and underestimate the power of marketplace trends." At the very least, Tisone has the merit of being clear in these statements. It is not principles or "our professional opinions" that will determine the structure and purpose of employee assistance but "marketplace forces." But, again, one must ask: Based on this criterion only, what would Tisone not include under the heading of employee assistance? What could not be included? Nothing, it seems, and this brings us back to the issue raised by Paul Roman and one that we discussed in Chapter 1: the issue of principles and the problem of knowledge. By definition, a principle is exclusive as well as inclusive; it tells us what the concept, idea, or issue is about, that is, what is essential to that principle, that without that the principle would not be that principle, but by so doing it also tells us what is not essential. Without principles, it is impossible to know what distinguishes one particular object or entity from other objects or entities. Thus, to say that marketplace forces, however these may be defined or described, will determine the structure and purpose of employee assistance is tantamount to saying that employee assistance can be anything anyone wishes to make it. This is a form of intellectual relativism that, like moral relativism, denies that it is ever proper or appropriate to say no.

Tisone's contempt for principles is nowhere more in evidence than when in the same essay he disingenuously praises the Core Technology as developed by Terry Blum and Paul Roman and then proceeds to dismiss it as irrelevant: "I want to emphasize the tremendous value which Paul Roman and Terry Blum's 'Core Technology' concept has added to our profession. It has given us a solid grounding from which to establish our minimum criteria for EAP legitimacy. It has offered a viable guideline for the many alternative approaches to EAP being generated in an ever-changing marketplace." The key phrase in the last sentence in this passage is "the many alternative approaches to EAP being generated in an ever-changing marketplace"; here Tisone makes clear that he has no interest in employee assistance as it is defined by the Core Technology, that employee assistance is only one approach among many, and that it is only "the many alternative approaches to EAP" that compel his interest.

If ever there was any doubt about Tisone's disdain for the Core Technology, the following statements should put that doubt to rest: "But the core technology does not drive the marketplace. I have yet to hear prospective clients or benefit consultants demand 'core technology' in a Request for Proposal (RFP). Increasingly, the market is asking for quality, accountability, cost effectiveness, and integration of EAP with mental health benefit management. Those who can deliver (and demonstrate it) are awarded contracts and jobs. And this is the primary dynamic which continues to shape our field." These words characterize the posture of one who is unwilling to engage the terms of the debate; indeed, they are simply dismissive and supercilious. To begin with, it is hard to believe that Tisone does not know why the Core Technology was developed, but based on his own words it must be assumed that he doesn't. The Core Technology was not designed to "drive the marketplace"; it was designed to define the principles and structure of a profession. Absent the Core Technology, there is no such thing as employee assistance. Just as every profession—the law and medicine, for example—has an essential set of core principles—its own "core technology"—that define and structure the profession, so too employee assistance. Perhaps another way of saying this is that every profession has a "core technology" that defines and describes the principles and activities of that profession and marks it off as that profession and not another. But one seeks the services of an attorney or a physician because one has a legal problem or a medical problem, respectively, and not because one is interested in the structure and principles of the profession. So too does an organization seek the services of an employee assistance program to help resolve particular kinds of problems that arise in the worksite. And when Tisone talks about quality, accountability, and cost-effectiveness, is he suggesting that employee assistance programs, that is, programs based on the Core Technology, were not providing these? At the very least, this is the implication in his words.

But there is an even more pertinent issue here, one that Tisone alludes to but does not spell out, and that is the issue of who benefits from the integrated program that he believes is the wave of the future. Tisone's words about quality, accountability, and cost-effectiveness to the contrary notwithstanding, there is another question that must be asked: When he states that "[t]hose who can deliver (and demonstrate it) are awarded contracts and jobs," and that this "is the primary dynamic which continues to shape our field," is he suggesting that the benefits of an integrated MMHC/EAP program are to be measured only or primarily by the program's ability to create "contracts and jobs" for those who administer such programs, and that this, and not the effort to resolve workplace problem situations or contain the costs of mental health care benefits, is "the primary dynamic" that does and ought "to shape our field"? For all of Tisone's words about the advantages accruing to the "EAP-driven" integrated program, there is no question that employee assistance, that is, employee assistance grounded firmly in the core technology, which is to say, a principled employee assistance, is not very high on his agenda. Indeed, the more one reads Tisone's words, the more employee assistance fades into insignificance.

Moreover, if the criteria for program effectiveness are quality, accountability, and cost-effectiveness, how are these criteria defined? How are they measured? Are they defined and measured solely by a reduction in the costs of mental health care benefits? By an increase in productivity? Both? Finally, what is the evidence that an integrated MMHC/EAP program can provide greater quality, accountability, and cost-effectiveness than an employee assistance program? What we have here is a series of assertions couched in abstraction. Tisone reminds one of nothing so much as the ideologue, she who has a blueprint for utopia and is not at all reluctant to claim that all sorts of benefits will ensue from the implementation of the blueprint. But when one examines the blueprint closely, one discovers that the benefits accrue primarily if not exclusively to the designer of the blueprint and not to the alleged beneficiaries.

Later in the same essay, Tisone returns to the issue of the Core Technology. "Frankly, I do not believe that maintaining responsiveness to the marketplace requires us to abandon 'core technology' as a basic EAP benchmark . . . but that does not mean that we must lock ourselves into a narrow band of EAP activity to preserve our professional dignity. To refuse to change and grow with the reality of the outside world (the marketplace) surely is the death-knell for the 'purists'." Like much of his writing, this passage makes very little sense and is marked by the same kind of disingenuousness. What does it mean to describe the Core Technology as a "basic EAP benchmark"? A benchmark for what? To determine what? And in view of Tisone's belief in the primacy of marketplace requirements, what role does the benchmark play? The fact is that the entire substance of Tisone's writings is designed to disparage traditional employee assistance principles, especially the Core Technology, and in their place put something that is entirely the creature of the marketplace. To state that "[t]o refuse to change and grow with the reality of the outside world (the marketplace)" marks one as a purist is to suggest that employee assistance as defined by the Core Technology is no more than a relic and those who espouse it mere reactionaries. Indeed, to describe those who disagree with him as purists is to suggest that they are out of contact with reality and as such deserving of little or no consideration. This, too, characterizes the stance of the ideologue. Moreover, to suggest, as he does, that adherence to principles, in this case, the Core Technology, is no more than an effort to "preserve our professional dignity," is to suggest that principles are simply irrelevant. I know of no one who adheres to principles merely to preserve her professional dignity; one adheres to the principles of a profession in order to preserve the ethical and substantive structure of that profession, and by so doing render services that are in the best interests of clients.

That same supercilious tone is present in Tisone's "Forward" to Dale

Masi's 1994 book, *Evaluating Your Employee Assistance and Managed Behavioral Care Program*: "By the mid 1980's, the mystique of the EAP counselor was vanishing faster than self-referrals to an alcohol-only EAP. Companies such as International Business Machines Corporation (IBM) were creating programs to address the needs of specific employee populations and could not accept nebulous references to 'problem improvement.' They wanted scientifically-based, medically-acceptable substantiation of program effectiveness both on a clinical and customer satisfaction basis. Increasingly, EAPs came under the microscope of various attempts to evaluate and quantify results. The paradigm of counselor as 'artiste' was doomed" (vii–viii).

Again, we are faced with the same dilemma; since Tisone does not tell us what he means by words and phrases such as "scientifically-based," "medically acceptable," and "quantify results," we are left with another series of airy abstractions. Upon what science is managed mental health care based? Who decides what is medically-acceptable? What does "medically-acceptable" mean? And what kinds of "results" are being quantified? Is it dollar amounts? Increases in productivity? These words and phrases are every bit as nebulous as the "problem improvement" Tisone derides as one of the deficiencies of EAPs. But there is an even more significant issue here—one that is buried deeply in Tisone's words and one that is the source of a great deal of mischief, and that is the issue of what constitutes science. It is not at all unusual today to hear people—for example, those in advertising—say that something is "scientifically proven" or "scientifically demonstrated" when in fact all they are voicing is opinion. To say that something is scientifically proven is more often than not merely a way to trump your opponent in debate; invoking the invincible aura of science is frequently an attempt to numb the critical faculty and still debate or disagreement. Similarly, when one describes quantification as scientific, it is no more than to suggest that numbers, in and of themselves, possess an all-encompassing kind of explanatory power. But this is not science; it is usually no more than addition. My point simply is that what Tisone is talking about when he uses words like "scientifically-based" is not science but *scientism,* one aspect of which is the notion that all human problems are technical problems, thus amenable to technical solutions. Scientism is pervasive, especially in the social sciences. As we will see a little later in this chapter, scientism and its progeny, technique, reign supreme in many areas of American life, including managed mental health care.

Like Tisone, Dale Masi is a proponent of the integrated MMHC/EAP model, but unlike Tisone she is at least willing to engage the terms of the debate and address the risks inherent in such a model. In her 1994 book, *Evaluating Your Employee Assistance and Managed Behavioral Care Program,* published by the Performance Resource Press, she states: "The channeling of services through a managed system oriented to financial responsibility and quality care also raises some organizational and political concerns. Like HMOs, managed care can allow financial factors to override diagnostic ones so that less than quality care delivered by less than qualified practitioners becomes an increasing problem. . . . Excellence and low costs are rarely compatible. . . . If the system becomes only a cheaper way of delivering services without regard to clearly defined evaluation mechanisms, quality care is lost" (28). If I am reading Masi correctly, she is very much aware that the potential for problems related to quality in an integrated model is very great indeed. And when she states that "[e]xcellence and low costs are rarely compatible," she is stating a self-evident truth. Masi also outlines with incomparable clarity and some specificity the essential differences between employee assistance and managed mental health care; her remarks are worth quoting at length (29):

a. EAPs obtain clients through supervisory trainings and employee outreach education. The focus of the EAP is on prevention and education, while MBC programs assume a more reactive approach, acting after a problem arises.

b. The EAP is a service model of increased usage defining an effective program. The fee structure is a fixed amount based on the total number of employees. Therefore, the client company pays the same amount regardless of employee use. The EAP looks for more clients. The MBC company does not, as this would raise the cost of the mental health budget.

c. The primary orientation for MBC programs is to reduce costs. MBC programs do not seek clients because their fee structure is on a per client basis. Therefore, each client costs the client company more money. While EAPs have been insulated from costs and viewed as the "warm fuzzy programs," MBC programs have been insulated from need.

d. EAPs are based on a social model to encompass family, community, and other issues such as work, childcare, and eldercare whereas the MBC is strictly a medical model. EAPs are concerned with employee and employer interdependence as well as the endemic problems of the organization. MBC is concerned only with the individual. In addition to addictions, EAPs are concerned with broader issues such as downsizing, cultural diversity, and literacy training. EAPs are concerned with organizational development, while MBC is concerned with clinical service.

By way of summary, Masi states: "The limitations of the integrated model are that it may concentrate too greatly on the benefits, to the loss of what else EAPs have traditionally done. Health care reform could cover the former and leave the integrated model with no 'meat on its bones'." But despite her very acute perceptions of the problems inherent in the integrated model, Masi insists that "[t]he role of EAPs . . . will be stronger than ever and fill the gaps left from the reform package" (33). This, essentially, is the message of her book.

For a number of reasons, it is difficult to reconcile Masi's support for the integrated model with her awareness of the problems endemic to that model. By her own admission, managed mental health care and employee assistance have very different ends or purposes, thus, it seems, the only way they could be integrated would be to strip employee assistance of its traditional functions, including the Core Technology, and reduce it to the role of gatekeeper for the managed mental health care program, which, in fact, is what has happened in many if not most integrated programs. In effect, employee assistance, at least as it is defined by the Core Technology, disappears. This is the only logical conclusion one can arrive at, based on Masi's own words. Indeed, at one time, just nine years prior to the publication of her book, this was also her conclusion. In an article entitled "Program Standards: Can We Ever Agree?" in the Winter 1985/86 issue of the *Employee Assistance Quarterly*, Herman L. Diesenhaus cites remarks made by Masi at an ALMACA conference and reprinted in *The Almacan* (1984): "If Employee Assistance Programs are not careful, they will be blended in the workplace with health promotion and stress programs and their purposes will be more clouded. . . . Do I think it is a negative kind of development? Yes, I do, because I think Employee Assistance Programs should not be so diluted that their identity is lost. In my opinion, the uniqueness of the Employee Assistance Program is the fact that personal problems have been tied to job performance and that the supervisor and unions have been referral sources" (9).

This is not to suggest that consistency is always and everywhere desirable; it is, however, to suggest that the dilution Masi feared in 1984 has in fact become a reality, aided and abetted by Masi herself. All of this raises an important question: Why talk at all about integrated models when we could simply do away with employee assistance and endorse a stand-alone straightforward managed behavioral health care (BHC) program? Or is it the case, as Tisone suggests, that managed mental health care programs offer an EAP merely to compete effectively in the marketplace. Then there is the issue of organizational development that, as Masi admits, is central to employee assistance and that would be costly to an integrated program where, protestations notwithstanding, short-term cost-effectiveness is its reason for being. Organizational development includes, among other things, such functions as supervisor training, employee orientation, and consultation with management at all levels, functions that are both costly and time consuming, at least in the short run. How does the integrated program allow for efforts such as these? Then there is the question of integrating two essentially dissimilar entities: How, specifically, is this to be done? Masi states that "the amalgamation of the two approaches can be problematic," since in addition to the administrative procedures required by managed mental health care programs, "the original EAP mandate must be maintained." However, "[t]he merging of the two systems does not simply mean combining them in their present forms. Changes will need to be made" (28). Here we are—finally—at the very heart of the problem: On the one hand, Masi tells us "that the original EAP mandate must be maintained," and, on the other, that "[c]hanges will need to be made." But what changes? Changes in the EAP? Changes in the managed mental health care program? In both? And how will the "original EAP mandate" be maintained in the integrated program? Other than to say that "[t]he merging of the two systems does not simply mean combining them in their present forms," she does not tell us. And although Masi does provide us with a model (30) of an integrated program, models tend to disintegrate when confronted with reality. How, for example, does an EAP maintain its original mandate in a system that is focused entirely on short-term cost-effectiveness?

For all of these reasons, it is important to focus precisely on what Masi is saying as well as what she is not saying. Unless one is a thoroughgoing Hegelian enamored of abstract synthesis, that is, the integration of objects fundamentally different from one another (at a high enough level of abstraction one can synthesize or amalgamate all sorts of essentially different objects, but only at the cost of obliterating the unique and essential qualities of those particular objects), integration or synthesis of different objects can take place only when those objects have some fundamental principle or axiom in common. Employee assistance, for example, can easily be reconciled or integrated with a conflict resolution or mediation model because both are designed to resolve conflicts or problem situations in the workplace, a form of risk management, or with a management training program (in addition to EAP supervisor training) because both contribute to organizational development.

This is not, however, the case with employee assistance and managed mental health care. As Masi herself seems to suggest, they have very little in common and are, in fact, if not irreconcilable, designed to do different things. To see that this is so, let's review again Masi's own comments on the differences between the two programs. When she states that "MBC programs do not seek clients," because doing so would increase costs, what she is saying, implicitly but nonetheless clearly, is that the MBC considers the client a *liability*. Indeed, she could not be considered otherwise; every client of an MBC represents a net loss for the program because the measure of its financial success is determined by its ability to deny or restrict services. There is no gainsaying this simple fact. It is an enormous intellectual stretch to suggest that a client who is viewed as a liability would be assessed or evaluated in a manner conducive to her best interests or would receive quality care. Nothing— neither the mechanisms for program evaluation suggested by Masi in her book nor claiming that managed care is "scientifically-based" will obviate that fact.

On the other hand, when Masi states that EAPs are concerned with "employee and employer interdependence" and "organizational development," what she is saying, again implicitly but also clearly, is that for employee assistance the client is an *asset*. Because the client is not merely a client but an individual whose behavior is influential within a context, she will have an effect on others within that context, that is to say, on organizational development. Put another way: For the EAP, the client's difficulties frequently become difficulties for those within the same context and possibly even beyond. For this reason, as Masi herself states, "The focus of the EAP is on prevention and education, while MBC programs assume a more reactive approach, acting after a problem arises." To the extent, then, that the EAP can help a troubled employee, to that extent it contributes to organizational well-being, hence the EAP perception of the troubled employee as an asset and its desire to be available to her.

Thus, other than through some dialectical sleight-of-hand, it is difficult to understand how the client-as-asset and the client-as-liability can be reconciled, for once we clear away all the verbiage, pro and con, this, ultimately, is the central issue. The client cannot be both an asset and a liability at the same time; she will be one or the other but not both. From a more general perspective, the issue of an integrated EAP/BHC model is merely a specific instance of that peculiarly modern desire to have it both ways at the same time or, in the colloquial version, to have one's cake and eat it too. It is a state of mind that, if it is not throwing temper tantrums, denies the limitations inherent in all of life and in all human endeavors. No matter how one views the issue, then, the conclusion is in every instance the same: Employee assistance and managed mental health care cannot be integrated without destroying employee assistance, hence it is difficult to understand how Masi arrives at the conclusion that the integrated model will make EAPs "stronger than ever." If short-term cost-effectiveness and the profits entailed in denying or restricting services are the deciding, indeed, the exclusive factors, and there is every reason to believe that in the integrated model they are, then the EAP, by the very nature of its end or purpose and its altogether different focus, will be emasculated, because it has no reason for being. Take employee assistance out of the worksite, attenuate its roots in the worksite in any way, and it no longer exists. Again, Masi's words are instructive: "The limitations of the integrated model are that it may concentrate too greatly on the benefits, to the loss of what else EAPs have traditionally done." Given the nature and purpose of managed mental health care and the nature of human nature, how could it be otherwise?

One suspects that Masi's integrated model is based on wishful thinking, however well-intentioned. The indisputable fact is that managed mental health care and employee assistance are essentially incompatible. The exclusive purpose of managed mental health care is to reduce health care costs, thus the emphasis on restricting and limiting services. The exclusive purpose of employee assistance is resolving workplace problems, which may mean, in the short run at least, increasing expenditures with an eye to reducing them in the long run. While managed mental health care seeks to contain costs immediately and in the short run, employee assistance seeks to reduce costs in the long run by helping the organization increase productivity. Cost savings, in other words, are a by-product of resolving problem situations in the workplace, thereby increasing productivity. Another way of saying this is that while employee assistance is designed to intervene in and alter the dynamics of the worksite, which means always being cognizant of the context, managed mental health care is designed to make access difficult and the context negligible.

In managed mental health care the burden of proof is on the client to demonstrate need; in employee assistance the burden of proof is on the EAP to demonstrate competence in resolving worksite problems that are costly for the organization. Unlike managed mental health care, employee assistance reaches out to the troubled employee and her supervisor, in which case it is only by denying the worksite-based nature and consulting function of employee assistance that the two can be integrated. In short, integration can take place only at the expense of the employee assistance program.

Perhaps another way of saying all of this—and for those in the employee assistance field who wish to see the field maintain its roots in the worksite, this is the crucial point—is that the integrated model, given the

byproduct of the managed care concept. For the first time the purchaser, the manager of care, and the provider are working together to ensure quality and cost-effective care for the user" (73).

And so it goes with the proponents of managed mental health care. Over and over again we are assured that managed mental health care is cost effective while at the same time providing quality of care for the user. We are also assured—"Ideally" at least—that in the integrated program the EAP will not be a junior partner but will, in fact, have an active, equal, and prominent role. But no matter how carefully one reads the interviews one cannot discern any role for the EAP other than that of "gatekeeper" for managed mental health care in the integrated program. Despite qualifying words and phrases such as "Ideally" and "we prefer" and despite efforts to take the sharpest edges off the word "gatekeeper" by using words like "facilitator" and "expeditor," employee assistance in integrated programs serves only one purpose: to reduce mental health costs by denying or restricting services. When, for example, Dolan, in the passage cited above, states that "[t]he EAP serves as a gatekeeper in the managed care system in the sense that it stops unnecessary referrals," and then attempts to muddy the waters by suggesting that we dispose of the word "gatekeeper" because it "carries a negative stigma" and "represents the EAP as a restrictive entity," he is, wittingly or unwittingly, playing word games. If the EAP is there to stop "unnecessary referrals"—whatever "unnecessary referrals" means—then it *is* "a restrictive entity," and no amount of dissembling—such as using words and phrases like "facilitator" or "expeditor" or "gate of access"— will change that. Besides the obvious corruption in the use of language in so much of the literature of managed mental health care, there is a great deal of wooly-headed thinking, and it's a good bet that the corruption came before the wooly-headed thinking.

Of the six people mentioned above who were interviewed, only Lee Wenzel goes right to the heart of the matter of the relationship between employee assistance and managed mental health care when he states: "Either EAPs will become cost conscious and cost accountable or HMOs and other medical management providers will take away all discretion from the EAP in selecting providers. If managed care programs that control provider selection also move into employer services, such as management consultation and training, there is really little function left for the EAP except to be a watchdog" (68). Wenzel's words have at least the merit of clarity. Here the mask is off, and we see the real face of managed mental health care; here there is no mention of equality between employee assistance and managed mental health care in an integrated program; here there is no suggestion that an integrated program will be "EAP-driven"—quite the reverse; here there is no mention of quality of care—the emphasis, rather, is on cost consciousness and cost account- ability; and here, finally, is the essence of managed mental health care—it is the one right way to achieve the maximum degree of cost- effectiveness in mental health care. Wenzel's words speak to the domi- nance of managed mental health care in any partnership between the latter and employee assistance. The clear implication in Wenzel's words is that managed mental health care and employee assistance have differ- ent ends or purposes and that employee assistance, if it wishes to avoid extinction, had better fall in line with the ends or purposes of managed mental health care. Perhaps the best proof of that assertion—if Wenzel's words are not convincing—is that rarely in the interviews is there any mention of traditional EAP functions such as supervisor training, or con- sultation with management, nor is there any mention of the prominent role of management in working with the troubled employee.

The reason is not hard to find: Far and away the most pronounced refrain in the literature of managed mental health care is the reduction or containment of the costs associated with mental health care. Indeed, this is the end—the only end—of managed mental health care; this is the reason for its birth and the engine that drives the entire process. And for this reason the proponents of managed mental health care cannot afford to entertain any proposition that even temporarily or minimally takes the focus off short-term cost reductions. This is the real message in Tisone's efforts to minimize the importance of the Core Technology: For the proponents of managed mental health care, the Core Technology and all that it suggests—grounding the EAP in the worksite by helping managers assimilate the principles and practice of employee assistance— is far removed from the objectives of managed mental health care. These are two entirely different worlds, and verbal sleights-of-hand will not change that simple fact. Moreover, what the evidence—or more pre- cisely, the lack of evidence—of the past decade shows is that claims for quality of care in managed mental health care programs are largely mythical.

In order to understand the confusion in the field, we have to look closely at the nature of managed mental health care. It is not enough merely to condemn it, as some of its antagonists do; we must, rather, ask why the nature of managed mental health care has nothing in com- mon with—indeed, it is hostile to—not only employee assistance but mental health care itself. The answer to our query lies in the meaning of the word "manage." When we seek to manage anything, what we are suggesting is the notion of control; we are stating that we wish to control the direction of the object, entity, or circumstance in question. Now, if the ends or purposes of the people doing the controlling are in accord with the ends or purposes intrinsic to or inherent in the thing being managed, there is no conflict. This is the case, for instance, with a doctor and her patient, where both are attempting to manage the patient's care in the direction of a favorable outcome or at least a diminution of the worst effects of the illness. And the reason why there is a convergence of interests in this case is that both the doctor and the patient are impelled by the *nature* of the illness itself and the process of recovery. Perhaps another way of understanding this is that when we seek to manage anything, we need to ask ourselves a simple but pointed question: Are the ends or purposes of the people doing the managing the same as or identical with the ends or purposes of the thing being managed? We need to distinguish between what may be two different, or at least potentially different, sets of interests—the ends or purposes of the people doing the managing and the nature of the thing being managed. If, for example, a government seeks to "manage" the news—a common occurrence in our world today, even in this country—then it's a good bet that the government's purpose is to put forth a version of the news that is at variance with the actual events themselves. The point here is that the integrity of the thing being managed will be preserved only if the management of that thing is derived from the nature, that is, the ends, purposes, or imperatives of the thing itself. This in turn implies a knowledge of and *obedience* to the nature of that particular object, entity, or process. All this means is that if we are desirous of maintaining our integrity or the integrity of anything external to ourselves, we must conform our thinking and our behavior to objective reality. This is the ancient and perennial notion of truth, and this is what is meant by obedience, the indispensable starting point in our quest for knowledge or truth. The question for us, then, is this: Are the ends or purposes of managed mental health care the same as or in accord with the ends or purposes of mental health care? Or, to put the question a slightly different way: Is managed mental health care cognizant of, knowledgeable about, and obedient to the nature of mental health care? Once we ask this question, it is no longer enough merely to assert that managed mental health care preserves the quality of mental health care while containing or reducing costs. So far at least, I have not seen anything in the literature that would lead me to believe that managed mental health care has any interest in the nature of mental health care. This brings us to our second consideration of managed mental health care.

As I suggested above, it is important to understand that managed mental health care is not mental health care. This statement may appear to be excessively repetitive, but it is crucial to understanding managed mental health care. When we speak of managed mental health care, then, it is important to be cognizant of the fact that for the proponents of managed mental health care it is the imperatives of the latter and not mental health care that are paramount, and this cannot be said too often. Whether managed mental health care programs are denying or restricting services or encouraging referrals to system programs or providers, the benefits accrue primarily to the entrepreneurs of such programs. This is the reason why one will find all sorts of references to technique or, more precisely, techniques—case management, utilization review, provider panels, and so on—in the literature but will look in vain for any reference to the nature of mental illness or mental health care or how managed mental health care addresses these. And the reason is not far to find: All of the techniques of managed mental health care are designed to affect costs, not produce quality. At this point I would like to digress briefly once more and explore the moral and intellectual roots of the present disorder in employee assistance, for those roots, while encompassing much more than employee assistance, go a long way toward explaining why the field is in the predicament it is, and why also David Sharar and William White are right to point to the ethical problems in the field.

As I noted above, employee assistance is not unique in the larger scheme of things. It is subject to the same kinds of influences affecting other institutions in our society; the upheavals and confusion in the employee assistance field today merely mirror what is happening with other institutions in the larger society. Confusion is ubiquitous, and change is the only absolute. Change, as the word is used in our modern lexicon, is merely a shorthand way of disposing of standards, principles, norms, values, and beliefs, especially if these are obstacles, or even potential obstacles, to that which is designated as, or proclaimed to be, better, greater, more efficient, and so on, than that which presently exists. To view change as always and everywhere a good is merely another way of foreclosing on the process of discursive reasoning. It is also the major concept in the vocabulary of ideologues. But the frenetic pursuit of change for the sake of change is perhaps the best evidence that we do no know where we want to go or why, and in order to assure ourselves that we're not whistling in the dark, we call this motion and activity progress.

That is just one side of the coin; the other side—and the two are intimately related—is a cultural ethos that denies the validity of all standards and principles and suggests that the past has nothing to offer us. Words like "tradition" and "authority," not to mention "humility," are anathema to us; they smack of control and restraint, a kind of brake on our desires and expectations, hence frustrating. In short, we live in an age of moral and intellectual relativism that not only leaves individuals rootless but the community in tatters. And the reason for this state of affairs is not hard to find: The problem for the moral and intellectual relativist is that since she has no principles, standards, or norms—that is, no capacity for discrimination, no means of distinguishing the true from the false—she can never say no. It is precisely this inability to say no that is the root of the problem, for if she cannot say no then everything, every idea, notion, whim, and hallucination—however contradictory, nonsensical, or repugnant to common sense—must be admitted into the community of discourse on an equal basis and without qualification. At the very least, the result is a kind of moral and intellectual numbness that leaves the relativist easy prey for the ideologue who comes armed with absolute certainty and finds it easy to make her home rent-free in the relativist's head.

Paralleling and reinforcing the absence of standards and principles, and both cause and effect of that absence, is the notion of absolute personal or individual autonomy, the idea that it is the individual who is the fountainhead of all wisdom, the court of last resort, and the final arbiter of all values. This is the essence of moral relativism; it is a view of the moral order that sees the latter as not only arbitrary and contingent but also egalitarian in that one view or belief is as good as any other, and no one belief or set of beliefs has any claim to superiority or priority. There is no ethical, moral, or cultural bond that unites people, or at least most people, in a community.

Relativism, then, whether of the moral or intellectual kind—ultimately, the two are the same—is a species of nihilism, the doctrine that there is no objective ground of truth and that all we can rely on is our own individual resources for making sense of our lives and the world. There are no overarching truths, no inclusive moral or intellectual framework, by which we can locate ourselves or to which we can look for guidance. In what may well be one of the premier works of moral philosophy in the latter half of the twentieth century, *After Virtue: A Study in Moral Theory,* Alasdair MacIntyre points to the implications for human life in such a theory: "The specifically modern self, the self that I have called emotivist [i.e., relativist], finds no limits set to that on which it may pass judgment for such limits could only derive from rational criteria for evaluation and, as we have seen, the emotivist self lacks any such criteria. Everything may be criticized from whatever standpoint the self has adopted, including the self's choice of standpoint to adopt" (31). Or, as MacIntyre suggests: "the peculiarly modern self . . . in acquiring sovereignty in its own realm lost its traditional boundaries provided by a social identity and a view of human life as ordered to a given end" (34).

But the loss of "limits," or a "social identity," or "a view of human life as ordered to a given end," is merely preliminary; it does no more than set the stage for what is to follow: social and moral isolation. MacIntyre puts it this way: "the price paid for liberation from what appeared to be the external authority of traditional morality was the loss of any authoritative content from the would-be moral utterances of the newly autonomous agent. Each moral agent now spoke unconstrained by the externalities of divine law, natural teleology, or hierarchical authority; but why should anyone now listen to him?" (68). Indeed, why should anyone else now listen to him? Given the lack of any common referent, any agreed-upon moral or conceptual framework, any standard to which he could appeal for even the smallest degree of certainty, the inevitable and invariable result will be social and moral isolation and the adoption of what can only be called a strategic mode of life. Again, MacIntyre: "Contemporary moral experience . . . has a paradoxical character. For each of us is taught to see himself or herself as an autonomous moral agent; but each of us also becomes engaged by modes of practice, aesthetic or bureaucratic, which involve us in manipulative relationships with others. Seeking to protect the autonomy that we have learned to prize, we aspire ourselves *not* to be manipulated by others; seeking to incarnate our own principles and standpoint in the world of practice, we find no way open to us to do so except by directing towards others those very manipulative modes of relationship which each of us aspires to resist in our own case. The incoherence of our attitudes and our experience arises from the incoherent conceptual scheme which we have inherited" (68).

The consequence of adopting a strategic mode of life is the will-to-power. In resisting the will of others and seeking to impose our own will, we have recourse only to power, which in the short run may gain for us what we desire but that inevitably and in the long run isolates us further, for the only result of the will-to-power can be wills in perpetual conflict. Perhaps another way of saying this is that absent some degree of moral and intellectual certainty in the social order, the way is open for the unscrupulous use of power to achieve morally and intellectually dubious ends. There is, in other words, an intimate and necessary relationship between the absence of moral and intellectual restraint, on the one hand, and the emergence of a potentially destructive power, especially that species of power we call technique, on the other. For the essence of power, as MacIntyre suggests, is manipulation, and manipulation, in turn, is the essence of technique. It is this which is at the root of the ethical improprieties Sharar and White describe so well in integrated managed mental health care systems, and it is this which precludes even the smallest degree of unanimity in ethical discourse.

If MacIntyre has given us the essential moral and intellectual dilemma in broad strokes, Peter Kreeft, in his book *Back to Virtue*, addresses the issue directly, suggesting that modernity has turned Aristotle upside down: "Long ago, Aristotle taught that there are three reasons for seeking knowledge. The most important one is truth, the next is moral action, and the last and least important is power, or the ability to make things: technique, technology, know-how" (21). What Kreeft is saying is that modernity, because it has abandoned the idea of any transcendent normative prescription, that is, truth, is incapable of initiating any kind of moral action, for moral action issues from truth, and is therefore left only with power or technique. And there is no question that ours is an age of enormous technical power and possesses an almost infinite number of techniques for manipulating nature, including human nature. But there's the rub: What principle, standard, truth, or prescription guides or restrains the use of that power and those techniques? Merely to ask the question indicates the depth of the problem. Again, I must emphasize that I am not arguing against progress, change, or technology; nor am I suggesting that the problem is technique itself or that technique in and of itself is wrong or diabolical. Obviously it is not. What I am suggesting is that the use of power, especially that species of power we call technique, is first and foremost a moral issue, not a technical issue, and must, therefore, be subject to moral discernment or, at the very least, searching questions about ends or purposes. Nor am I under any illusion that this will be easy to do or indeed that there will be much interest in doing so, especially in an age of moral and intellectual relativism. The most potent conversation stopper at social gatherings when the conversation turns to moral issues is the question: Whose morality? But to ask that question is not a reason to end the conversation; rather, it should be the prelude to a vigorous and spirited debate about moral issues and the ends or purposes surrounding the application of power. For as Kreeft suggests, we have reached a point in human evolution where the more powerful we have become technologically, the weaker we have become in understanding the implications in the use of that power: "We control nature, but we cannot control our own control. We control nature, but we cannot or will not control ourselves. Self-control is 'out' exactly when nature control is 'in,' that is, exactly when self-control is most needed" (23). The result, Kreeft suggests, "is that *we* do not hold the power. More and more power over nature is placed in hands that are weaker and weaker." Weaker and weaker morally, that is. This is our dilemma, and our only response to it thus far is a greater refinement of our techniques. Indeed, so powerful has the drive to refine and use techniques become that some writers speak of "the technological imperative," meaning that technique has become an end in itself rather than a means to an end. It has no purpose other than the realization of its own imperatives; it would be easy enough to cite instances where a technology has been used merely because it was available, not because it was necessary or even desirable in achieving a particular end, and even when the application of that technology created problems greater than the one it was designed to resolve. Kreeft cites a passage from C. S. Lewis's *The Abolition of Man* to make this point: "There is something which unites magic and applied science [technology] while separating them from the 'wisdom' of earlier ages. For the wise men of old, the cardinal problem of human life was how to conform the soul to objective reality, and the solution was wisdom, self-discipline, and virtue. For the modern, the cardinal problem is how to conform reality to the wishes of man, and the solution is technique" (22). And Kreeft states, "I have never read any three sentences that go more deeply to the heart of our civilization and its distinctiveness than these."

Perhaps the best description of technique, which is unrestrained by any imperative other than its own, is that provided by Jacques Ellul in his *The Technological Society*. He defines technique in the following way: "The twofold intervention of reason and consciousness in the technical world, which produces the technical phenomenon, can be described as the quest of the one best means in every field. And this 'one best means' is, in fact, the technical means. It is the aggregate of these means that produces technical civilization" (21). Ellul also suggests that with the evolution of technology, technique has become more than a means; it has, in fact, become an end in itself: "Technical progress is no longer conditioned by anything other than its own calculus of efficiency. The search is no longer personal, experimental, workmanlike; it is abstract, mathematical, and industrial. This does not mean that the individual no longer participates. On the contrary, progress is made only after innumerable individual experiments. But the individual participates only to the degree that he resists all the currents today considered secondary, such as aesthetics, ethics, fantasy. Insofar as the individual represents this abstract tendency, he is permitted to participate in technical creation, which is increasingly independent of him and increasingly linked to its own mathematical law" (74).

What Ellul is saying here is that technique has become an end in itself; it is restrained by no imperatives other than its own, and its quest is for its own perfection, which is to say, the maximum degree of efficiency. Moreover, technique, as Ellul suggests, is essentially mathematical; it permits evaluation only on its own terms, that is, in terms of measurable units; it is pure quantification. And that which cannot be quantified is summarily rejected; that which is the least bit idiosyncratic or subjective, or that which is in any way given over to personal interpretation or whim is discarded in technique's relentless drive for its own perfection. There is, moreover, as Ellul suggests, an additional consideration when we speak of technique, and that is "that technique, in its development, poses primarily technical problems that consequently can be resolved only by technique. The present level of technique brings on new advances, and these in turn add to existing difficulties and technical problems, which demand further advances still" (92).

If these were the only or the most pernicious consequences of technical evolution, we might, with some justification, argue that in any costs/benefits analysis of technical civilization the benefits outweigh the costs, that on balance technical progress has been a boon rather than a bane. But there is another side to the equation, and this is the side that concerns Ellul and that he calls "self-augmentation": "The implications of self-augmentation become clearer: The individual's role is less and less important in technical evolution. The more factors there are, the more readily they combine and the more evident is the urgent need for each technical advance. Advance for its own sake becomes proportionately greater and the expression of human autonomy proportionately feebler." What Ellul is suggesting here is that the evolution of technique is in the direction of greater and greater autonomy, driven only by its own imperatives and in a progression that is geometrical rather than arithmetical. In effect, the individual himself becomes merely another technique amidst a proliferation of techniques. As Ellul suggests: "In this decisive evolution, the human being does not play a part. Technical elements combine among themselves, and they do so more and more spontaneously. In the future, man will apparently be confined to the role of a recording device; he will note the effects of techniques upon one another, and register the results" (93).

It takes only a few seconds' thought to realize that Ellul is not writing science fiction. One has only to look at the proliferation of efforts to escape the confines of an increasingly restrictive rational-technical civilization to know that Ellul has penetrated to the essence (a word that technique would banish from our lexicon) of our civilization. The extraordinary upsurge of mysticism, ersatz religious and quasi-religious groups, ideologies that are essentially religious in nature, such as radical environmentalism, among others, is testimony to the fact that ours has become an increasingly constrictive society, primarily because of an imperious technique that abhors anything that is not amenable to its drive for perfection. Whether, broadly, we call it New Age or the new religious sensibility, we are witnessing more and more irrational (irrational, that is, in a civilization given over to technical perfection) efforts to escape the confines of an increasingly monistic society.

It is important to note that although he is pessimistic about the future, Ellul is not anti-technology nor is he suggesting regression to a less technical society. In any case, we could not regress, at least not without catastrophic upheavals. What he is suggesting, and what his work is all about, is a much greater awareness of and greater clarity about the threats to civilization from the drive for technical perfection.

Technique, then, can be defined as manipulation in the service of achieving the greatest degree of efficiency possible. Moreover, technique can also be understood as a species of scientism, the doctrine (1) that science has the answer to *all* human problems, (2) that all human problems are essentially technical problems, and (3) that all human problems are, therefore, susceptible to technical solutions. In his *The Virtue of Civility,* Edward Shils defines scientism as "the belief that scientific methods and scientific knowledge could provide the basis for social engineering on a massive scale." "This belief—that the application of science could 'solve' social problems—affected a wide range of academic disciplines, and turned them into fortresses and arsenals of reform" (141). One does not have to look very far or for very long to find examples of scientism. It pervades government at all levels, even business, and especially education. A popular college textbook entitled *Management of Organizational Behavior: Utilizing Human Resources* by Kenneth H. Blanchard and Paul Hersey provides an explicit example of scientism. In a subsection entitled "Predicting Future Behavior," the authors tell us that "[a]lthough understanding past behavior is important for developing effective human skills, it is not enough by itself. If you are supervising other people, it is essential that you understand why they did what they did yesterday, but perhaps even more important is being able to predict how they are going to behave today, tomorrow, next week, and next month under similar as well as changing environmental conditions.

Therefore, the second level of expertise that managers need is predicting future behavior" (12). On page 14 the authors tell us that "[i]f managers are able to understand, predict, and direct change and control behavior, they are essentially applied behavioral scientists." And on the same page the authors tell us who and what a behavioral scientist is: "[A] behavioral scientist integrates concepts and theories and the results of empirical studies from the areas of cultural anthropology, economics, political science, psychology, sociology, and social psychology. At the same time, a behavioral scientist also borrows from other areas such as engineering, physics, quantitative analysis, and statistics. For example, force field analysis, developed by Kurt Lewin . . . is directly related to concepts in physics. So, perhaps the best way to look at the field is to say that a behavioral scientist attempts to integrate all of those areas or disciplines that can be useful to us as practitioners in understanding, predicting, and having an impact on the behavior of individuals and groups." O'Brien, one of the chief protagonists in George Orwell's *1984,* would have no trouble endorsing these passages.

This is pure scientism, or what some might call social engineering, but it is not science, behavioral or otherwise; it is technique dressed up in the jargon of science and intended to convey the notion that management is merely a matter of manipulating reality, that is to say, other people. This is also an attempt to clothe the uncertainty and unpredictability of human behavior in an aura of science, thereby suggesting that human behavior can be predicted and controlled. And this is also a good example of what happens when the social sciences try to emulate the methods of the natural sciences. But our authors do express a degree of ambivalence about their "science": "[I]t should be remembered that applied behavioral science is not an exact science such as physics, chemistry, and biology. There are no principles or universal truths when it comes to management. People are difficult to predict. All that the behavioral sciences can give you are ways to increase your behavioral batting average. In other words, the behavioral sciences are probability sciences. There aren't any principles of management, only books titled *Principles of Management*" (15).

Some of these statements are, to say the least, curious and not a little contradictory. To state that there "are no principles or universal truths when it comes to management" seems to contradict the notion that one can predict and control human behavior. And then to say that the behavioral sciences are really "probability sciences" is to suggest that they are not really sciences at all. Finally, to state that "there aren't any principles of management" would seem to undermine the entire thesis of the authors' book. Moreover, and this should be the area of greatest concern for those who are in management and those in the human services field, to suggest that there aren't any principles of management is to suggest that management is no more than pure technique, governed only by its own imperatives and heedless of all consequences other than its own perfection. And when we talk about predicting and controlling the behavior of others, we are saying that human beings are no more than objects to be manipulated. At this point we are on the threshold of totalitarianism.

In his brilliant book, *The Virtue of Civility*, Edward Shils takes us to the heart of scientism. "Scientism," he states, "entails the denial of the truth of tradition. It asserts that life, if it is to be lived on the highest plane, should be lived in accordance with 'scientific principles,' and that these principles should be achieved by the rigorously rational examination of actual experience, systematically confronted through the elaborate and orderly scrutiny and experiment which constitute scientific research. It regards the generally accepted traditions of society as impediments to the attainment of these principles, which are ultimately the principles immanent in the universe. As such, therefore, scientism constitutes a vigorous criticism of traditional and institutional life, and a refusal to accept authority on any grounds except those of scientific principle. It holds before mankind the ideal of a society in which scientists, and administrators and politicians guided by scientists, will rule and in which the ordinary citizens will hold no beliefs and perform no actions which are not sanctioned by scientific principles" (44). Thus the past or what we call tradition will have no voice in the creation of the new man and the new society. Rather, it will be "experts" in possession of the right techniques who will determine and control the thoughts and behavior of people and societies. In his recent book, *Plagues of the Mind: The New Epidemic of False Knowledge*, Bruce S. Thornton traces the origins of scientism to the eighteenth-century Enlightenment: "This Enlightenment faith in the power of reason to describe with scientific precision the mysteries of human identity was buttressed . . . by the belief that 'techniques' could be invented for changing it" (54). The implications are clear; as Thornton puts it: "social problems will become the domain of therapeutic 'experts,' who will need more and more coercive power— and less and less freedom on the part of recalcitrant individuals to make their 'solutions' work." Indeed, the age of the "experts" is already upon us; when Blanchard and Hersey talk about "applied behavioral science," they are talking about technique, and when they suggest to managers that they are "behavioral scientists," we are in the presence of "experts."

In short, "applied behavioral science" is no more than a euphemism for technique.

All of this may seem to be an unnecessarily circuitous route to take to understand the virus at the heart of managed mental health care and its impact on mental health care and on those employee assistance programs that have chosen to become part of managed mental health care programs. But it is, I believe, necessary to provide a context that will enable us to see and understand the subtle as well as not-so-subtle aspects of managed mental health care's approach to mental health care and the uses to which it would put employee assistance.

First of all, as I noted earlier, managed mental health care has no interest in mental health care, no interest in the nature and purpose of therapy, and indeed no interest in the nature of the problem the client brings to the therapist's office. It views the client as a liability and the therapist as a technician or a kind of "engineer of the mind" whose only purpose is to "fix" the client as quickly and as inexpensively as possible. Essentially what this means is that both the client and the therapist are at the mercy of the managed mental health care program, which is to say that all discretion about the therapeutic process is taken away from the therapist and the client and lodged in the hands of a managed mental health care consultant who may or may not be knowledgeable about the nature of therapy or the nature of mental illness but who nevertheless decides what the client and the therapist will do and how they will do it. In short, managed mental health care does not derive its criteria for care from the nature of mental health care; its focus is costs (or jobs, contracts, and dollars), and this is its only criterion.

Second, managed mental health care is a species of scientism; it views the practice of therapy solely and exclusively as a technical problem, the therapist as a technician, and the client as a problem to be solved. It has no interest in the intangible, the unquantifiable, or the highly subjective interaction between therapist and client. Thus managed mental health care would make the therapist herself a technique in the service of technique. Unfortunately, too many mental health professionals have succumbed to the lure of managed mental health care, either because it promises a degree of financial security or because they too see psychology and therapy as technical in nature.

In a very real sense, managed mental health care is a species of what the great Lutheran theologian Dietrich Bonhoeffer described as the doctrine of cheap grace, which is to say, the attempt to acquire virtue without effort, pain, or redemption. The proponents of the doctrine of cheap grace wished to be judged solely by their good intentions (the currently popular fad of wearing lapel ribbons to indicate support for various causes is just one example) and are forever proclaiming and promoting their own self-righteousness. The doctrine of cheap grace has become a substitute for the quest for truth and at the present time is pervasive in our society—we see it in the posturing of our political leaders, in our educational system (in the form of efforts to improve students' self-esteem), in the triumph of the therapeutic, and in the innumerable causes promoted by ideologues of one kind or another.

We see a variation of the doctrine of cheap grace at work in the employee assistance field today in the form of abstraction. One of the most noticeable features of institutions in a state of dissolution is abstraction, by that I mean that the less able an institution is in carrying out the function for which it was called into existence, the greater the tendency to and the need for increasingly higher levels of abstraction to provide the illusion of coherence, unity, and vitality. Even a cursory glance at any issue of the *Exchange* will provide sufficient evidence of that assertion. The roots of the problem are easy to discern: Once you abandon the idea that there is such a thing as truth, there are no longer any obstacles to the propagation of every and any kind of fantasy. Indeed, the very first task of any ideology is to deny reality, and the easiest way to do this is to posit an abstract realm in which there are no obstacles to our desires, that is, a realm in which there are no conflicts and no contradictions. This is where employee assistance is today, and it is also the reason why managed mental health care so easily assumed control of the profession.

When we speak of truth, then, we are speaking about that which corresponds to or is in accord with reality, and reality, ultimately, is concrete, particular, specific, and verifiable. This is not to deny the truth or reality of concepts, hypotheses, or theories, but these, if they are to be verifiable, must be anchored in the objectively real and, therefore, the knowable. Concepts, hypotheses, and theories that do not have their roots in reality are beyond verification, hence useless for the living of life or the acquisition of knowledge. Indeed, it is these—unverifiable concepts, hypotheses, and theories—which are the stuff of ideology. They are, in a very real sense, "immaculate conceptions," rootless abstract blueprints for some kind of utopia. And these have been the source of much of the horror of the twentieth century.

In essence, the difference between truth and "managed" truth is the same as the difference between mental health care and managed mental health care. In both instances, the adjective "managed" negates entirely that which is essential to an understanding of the entities under consideration; managed truth will be quite at variance with truth and managed mental health care quite at variance with mental health care, for one reason if for no other: The truth of truth and the truth of mental health care can be derived only from their correspondence with reality, not from the imposition of some externality driven only by considerations of cost or ideology. For once we impose any kind of externality foreign to the nature of an object or entity, we distort its nature. It becomes something other than what it was and is, consequently, unable to testify to the nature of things with any veracity. At this point we have a kind of cognitive dissonance. The best evidence for the truth of this last proposition is the increasing chorus of complaints about managed health care, wherein diagnoses and prognoses are given short shrift, provider recommendations ignored, and the only criterion given an audience is that of cost.

If this seems like an overly harsh indictment of managed mental health care, it might be well to ask ourselves a simple question: Is there a difference between managed mental health care and mental health care, that is, why do we call one managed and the other not? If the answer to the first part of that question is "yes," then we must ask another question: What is the difference? We might also look at the issue from another perspective: The success of a managed mental health care program is measured entirely in terms of cost, thus the lower the cost, the more successful (if that's the word) the program is. If we take this line of thought to its logical conclusion, we can say that a managed mental health care program will be considered successful to the degree that it reduces the costs of mental health care and completely successful if it incurs no costs at all. This is the inherent logic of managed mental health care, and no amount of talk about quality of care will change that logic one bit. Thus it is cost—and not the nature of mental health care or mental illness or provider recommendations—that will carry the day. To assume that the logic of managed mental health care can or will be modified by ritual incantation—such as "ensuring quality of care"—is not only to defy the nature of logic but to defy common sense.

But its exclusive focus on cost reduction or containment is only one of the troubling aspects of managed mental health care. Another aspect, one that we have already alluded to, is the obvious contempt shown by the proponents of managed mental health care and the integrated program for the principles and practice of employee assistance. Perhaps one of the most telling indictments of the arguments of the proponents of the integrated program is that rarely, if ever, do they address the nature and structure of the worksite, or the relationship between it and employee assistance. It is as if the worksite did not exist.

Nor, for the same reason, does management have any role in the integrated model. It is completely contradictory to say, on the one hand, that management is the medium that gives form and substance to an employee assistance program and, on the other, to reduce costs by denying or restricting services. Management can be the medium only if it has an active role to play in the implementation and maintenance of an EAP, and that role makes sense only within the context of employee assistance as a worksite-based management program. To eliminate or de-emphasize the contextual nature of employee assistance is to nullify the role of the manager and the principles and practice of employee assistance.

To see this from its broadest perspective, we must recall the function of employee assistance as a subsystem within a parent system. As an integrated component of the system, employee assistance is charged, first, with communicating to the employer and employee alike the relationship between impaired job performance, of whatever kind, and productivity and, second, instituting specific and concrete ways and means of resolving problem situations in the workplace. Such efforts include supervisor training, employee orientation to the EAP, consultation with supervisors, consultation and planning sessions with executive management, the development of policy statements, and case management, among others. Thus employee assistance, or at least a well-integrated employee assistance program, is itself a highly articulated system that is rooted in and circumscribed by the nature and structure of the worksite, charged with resolving worksite problems that adversely affect job performance and productivity, and committed over the long term and in the long run to organizational development. As a subsystem within a parent system, it is concerned with practice, which is to say, with standards. To repeat, if an employee assistance program is to be effective—and this is crucial to an understanding of employee assistance—it must be thoroughly integrated into and a function of the normative requirements of the organization.

Contrast this with managed mental health care, and the differences are immediately obvious. Because managed mental health care's immediate and sole interest is affecting cost savings and profits in the short run, it has little or no interest in problem situations in the workplace or, what is essentially the same thing, organizational development. In effect, it is a loosely attached appendage of the system rather than an integral part of it and is called into play only when health care situations with a potential for costs arise. It is neither integrated into nor does it have any interest in the normative requirements of the institution. Again, we will have one or the other—managed mental health care or employee assistance—but not both.

At the very least, Carr and McCann are candid and logically consistent when they openly seek to strip employee assistance of its essentials and make it a health care delivery system. In fact, the Carr-McCann thesis is, in its own way, the best proof of the incompatibility of managed mental health care and employee assistance. Recognizing that incompatibility, they sever employee assistance from the worksite with one stroke, without pretense, and without a host of tortured rationalizations.

The following is an actual portrayal of what happened to one EAP in my part of the country when it was "integrated" with a managed mental health care program. The person who was the director of that employee assistance program is a friend of mine who wishes to remain anonymous; he did, however, provide me with an unpublished document, the *Committee B Report,* which describes in some detail the disastrous consequences in a very short period of time for his program as the result of the merger. The merger was initiated in 1992 and ended in 1994.

This was a not-for-profit hospital-based EAP that at its peak serviced the hospital and 122 other organizations totaling some 28,200 employees and their family members. At the time of the merger the EAP had an income of $40,000 over and above its operating expenses. It is important to note, also, that my friend remained the director of the EAP during the period of the merger and for some time afterward. For the most part, I'll let him tell the story.

The first thing he learned shortly after the programs were integrated was that all decisions concerning treatment or therapy would be made by the staff of the managed care program, not by the staff of the employee assistance program, and that those decisions would be final (1). As he puts it: "One of my primary concerns was that the EAP was not given any opportunity to override decisions on treatment recommendations. Under the new system, we had to adhere to any denials on claims that the [managed care entity] desired and could not even make a treatment recommendation until we had consulted with their claims managers. The process put the two, [the] EAP and [the managed care entity], into a conflict of interests, goals, purposes, and ideology." This, after being promised prior to the merger that the two programs would enjoy equal status and that the managed care program would not encroach on the prerogatives of the EAP or seek to eliminate or modify traditional employee assistance principles and practice.

Shortly after the two programs were integrated, a letter (1–2) was sent "to all of our EAP companies informing them that we were now a 'for-profit' entity, merged with [a managed care program] and that in the next year or so we would be increasing our annual fees from 20–50%. This resulted in 18 companies (4,000+ employees) withdrawing from . . . the EAP immediately or at the end of their current contracts. [One company] withdrew stating that it was a conflict of interest for us to recommend services while our superiors could order us to deny such claims. Basically, all 18 companies felt that this was a violation . . . of their trust with [the EAP] because they had been sold on the concept of a 'free-standing EAP' and that had been withdrawn without any consultation with our companies. We were never able to reinstate any of these companies with our EAP at a later date. . . . At our bottom, we got down to between 16,000–18,000 employees and about 75–80 companies. It was at that time that the divorce did occur, but we never recovered our former strength because the community had lost its trust in our word."

And the litany goes on; the EAP staff was reduced from 6.5 FTE to 1.75 FTE while the managed care staff was increased. EAPs, which had been promised to companies, never materialized, and the integrated program lost 1.4 million dollars. It was that loss that brought about the dissolution of the integrated program after two years. I could go on (the document is single-spaced and seven pages long), but enough has been said already to indicate the kinds of problems inherent in attempting to integrate two essentially dissimilar entities. What had been a fundamentally sound and effective EAP was irrevocably damaged. I might add also that this is not an isolated case; I have personal knowledge of this and similar kinds of things happening with other integrated programs. In my part of the country at the present time, there are several integrated behavioral health care systems that base their marketing efforts on, among other things, the promise that if the prospective client organization buys their behavioral health care product they will also get an employee assistance program free of charge. To date, the promised EAPs have not materialized; instead, those companies that purchased the behavioral health care product got an 800 hot line and nothing more.

Managed mental health care, then, is no more than a technique designed to achieve the greatest degree of efficiency possible in reducing the costs of mental health care, on the one hand, and, on the other, insuring financial gains for the entrepreneurs of such programs. Indeed, the two are merely opposite sides of the same coin. Moreover, managed mental health care is a species of scientism, dressed up in the jargon of science and intended to convey an ideal of efficiency. And as is the case in all scientist efforts, the medium is technique, which, first of all, means the power to manipulate and implies such things as control, dominion, and the ability to exert force to achieve a given end. Second, in and of itself, technique does not entertain ethical or moral considerations; it is, rather, promiscuous and in the service of the highest bidder; it is neither moral nor immoral, but amoral. Third, technique acknowledges no ends, purposes, or imperatives other than its own. This is why, as Kreeft noted, Aristotle believed that technique must be guided by truth and its offspring, moral action. Fourth, technique is exclusive rather than inclusive; only those elements that support the realization of its ends will get an audience. Fifth, technique is imperious; it is designed to achieve absolute control, and this, incidentally, is why it is nonsense to talk about integrating managed mental health care and employee assistance, especially on the basis of anything resembling equality. The evidence is abundant that managed mental health care and employee assistance are essentially different from one another, that is, they have mutually exclusive ends, and that any "integration" will be done strictly on managed mental health care's terms. Sixth, technique is highly rationalized and abstract; it is content-less, thus easily applied to any given object, entity, process, or event in any number of ways; it is, in other words, a rational-technical means of manipulating reality. For all of these reasons, Sharar and White's proposal for an ethics summit ultimately misses the point: The universe of ethical discourse and the universe of scientism are diametrically opposed to one another. The first knows nothing of technique and the second nothing but.

We may summarize the foregoing in the following four propositions. These are features of managed mental health care that are not mentioned by its proponents, but they are features that must be understood if we are to make sense of the wholly pernicious consequences of attempting to subject mental health care to no other consideration than that of a spurious efficiency.

1. It is not health care or a health care delivery system. Indeed, it has no interest in health care; its sole purpose is the reduction of health care costs. This is its only reason for being.

2. It is a technique, and like all techniques, it is driven only by its own imperatives. It is not a means to an end—it is and constitutes an end in itself, which is its own perfection or the maximum possible degree of efficiency.

3. It is exclusive rather than inclusive; only those elements that lend themselves to efficient manipulation will be admitted into the system. Other kinds of considerations, such as those that are unique, those that appertain only to particular instances or individuals, or those that are the least bit idiosyncratic, will be excluded.

4. Like all techniques, it is imperious; it is designed to dominate and, left to its own devices, will tolerate no interference or deviation.

Managed mental health care is not mental health care, and employee assistance and managed mental health care have different and mutually exclusive ends. Employee assistance and managed mental health care are anything but "harmonious," and this is the reason why managed mental health care programs like to have an EAP fronting for them. The EAP is a kind of cosmetic overlay or camouflage designed to obscure the fact that managed mental health care is concerned only with costs, not with health care. By the rational-technical nature of its structure and purpose, managed mental health care is precluded from indicating any concern about health care as such or about ethical proprieties. Because it is a technique guided only by its own considerations, its focus is narrow and its end efficiency. Technique, mindful only of its own imperatives, is the essence of scientism and the virus at the heart of managed mental health care.

Finally, I would like to review EAPA's relationship to managed mental health care. In 1990, EAPA published a "monograph" entitled *EAP Solutions to the Employer Health Cost Crisis,* which is, to say the least, a curious document. It appears to endorse some combination of employee assistance and managed mental health care services but at the same time makes every effort to distance itself from managed mental health care by delineating the fundamental differences between the latter and employee assistance. On page 12 we find the following: "In determining how an EAP-managed behavioral health care system will function, an organization should consider the capabilities of its existing EAP. *The critical questions are what mix of EAP-managed behavioral health care services does a particular employer need and how many outside vendors are required to most efficiently provide those services* (italics in original). For an organization that purports to be the flagship and voice of employee assistance, these words take one's breath away. What does a "mix" of EAP-managed behavioral health care services mean? Does it mean that an organization is free to pick and choose those components of an integrated program that it wishes to implement while ignoring others? Does it mean that if an employer so chooses she can design a "mix" that eliminates one or more components of employee assistance? And what about the words "outside vendors"? Do they mean that the employee assistance program is no longer to be an integral part of the organization but merely a kind of external entity peddling an ill-assorted and incoherent medley of "services"? At best, to talk of a mix of services is disingenuous; at worst, it signals EAPA's complete and abject surrender to managed mental health care. With these words, EAPA, it seems, ran up the white flag.

But the problem has deeper roots, and these are the source of the confusion in the monograph. When the authors of the monograph speak of "an EAP-managed behavioral health care system," are they suggesting that the focus of employee assistance is now behavioral health care and not behavioral risk management? Are they suggesting that employee assistance is now, or should be, no more than a gatekeeper for managed behavioral health care, and does this in turn mean that the primary focus of employee assistance is now that of merely evaluating clients and making recommendations to the managed mental health care consultant as to the suitability of those clients for therapy, rather than that of resolving problem situations in the workplace? If so, employee assistance is acquiescing in its own dissolution.

Now consider the following statements, also from the monograph (10–11):

The goals of the managed behavioral health care system focus on the period of time the employee or dependent utilizes the medical benefits, while the goals of an EAP span the employee's entire career with the organization.

Managed behavioral health care services delivered on a stand-alone basis are often not very effective in controlling long term behavioral health care costs, for three reasons:

[1] Managed behavioral health care focuses exclusively on the period when an individual is in an acute or extended and expensive medical care episode. The individual intervention focus often overlooks sources of significant related health care expenditures, such as family and dependent medical expenses or medical diagnoses related to the behavioral health problem, which are not part of the acute episode. Thus, managed behavioral care misses the opportunities for prevention and early intervention which are the core of EAP services.

[2] Managed behavioral health care deals with only one aspect of the cost to the employer, the direct health care cost, while missing the opportunity to control indirect costs, such as absenteeism and/or attrition. These problems can only be addressed with a more comprehensive program such as EAP.

[3] Managed behavioral health care short-circuits the systematic planning and coordination of the variety of behavioral health management techniques required for the effective evaluation of

health care providers in favor of succeeding on only one measure—short-term costs. Quality health care must be evaluated in
terms of outcomes measured in years, not in days of hospitali-
zation for a particular episode.

To buttress its contention that EAPs are effective in controlling health
care costs, the monograph (7–8) cites several instances of the effectiveness of EAPs at various corporations, naming McDonnell Douglas, General Motors, Kimberly-Clark, and AT&T. I have no doubt the results are
impressive, and I for one am inclined to agree with the authors of the
monograph about the effectiveness of EAPs in controlling costs, but it
is that very same inclination that leads me to ask the following question:
Why, in view of these successful results, do the authors of the monograph
believe it necessary to endorse some "mix" of employee assistance and
managed behavioral health care? To put this question another way: Is it
not self-defeating for both employee assistance and the profession to
sacrifice the integrity of an apparently successful approach to resolving
problem situations in the workplace for a hybrid with its obvious deficiencies? And why do the authors of the monograph focus on behavioral
health care when the proper focus of employee assistance is the worksite
and its dynamics? One final question: Why, in view of the obvious deficiencies of managed behavioral health care as outlined in the monograph, do the authors bother to consider it at all? What is puzzling and,
indeed, disturbing about the monograph is that it manages to accomplish
two completely contradictory ends at the same time: On the one hand,
it outlines with incomparable clarity the deficiencies of managed mental
health care and, on the other, it promotes some mix of the latter and
employee assistance. To be sure, mind reading is always a dangerous
pastime, but since the authors of the monograph do not bother to tell us
what their motives were in writing the monograph, we will attempt to
infer at least some of them. Intimidation is always a causal factor in
influencing thinking and behavior; intimidated by pressure from several
different quarters to reduce health care costs, EAPA's leadership capitulated to demands that employee assistance become part of the effort to
reduce those costs. Fear is also a causal factor; fearful that employee
assistance would be sidelined by efforts to reduce health care costs,
EAPA decided to get on the bandwagon. Crumbs, it seems, are better
than starvation. Failure to act on principles is also a causal factor; such
failure always results in adverse consequences. And this may be the most
damning indictment of the profession's leadership: Unsure or uncertain
of the legitimacy of the principles of employee assistance, or desirous

of power and influence at the price of abrogating principles, EAPA's leadership took the expedient way out, apparently not realizing that ideas have consequences or that expediency is always a sure route to disaster, at least in the long run. EAPA, in short, actively participated in the dissolution of employee assistance.

The best words I can think of to describe the monograph, especially its tone, are nervousness, defensiveness, and ambivalence. When I first read it, and on subsequent readings, the thought that came to mind was that of the hostess of a party who reluctantly lets in an uninvited party crasher of dubious reputation and then spends the rest of the evening looking over her shoulder in an attempt to monitor her uninvited guest's behavior. This is no way to enjoy a party, and it certainly detracts from seeing to the needs of the other guests. My point simply is that the employee assistance field has no need to entertain the dubious pretensions of the managed mental health care industry. The solution is obvious: If employee assistance professionals will do what they know they should be doing, that is, implement employee assistance programs based firmly on the core technology, they will be successful in their endeavors. Not to do so will only encourage other party crashers.

Nine years later, nothing much had changed, or, more precisely perhaps, the field was continuing to exhibit the symptoms of dissolution. In the 1999 edition of the *EAPA Standards and Professional Guidelines for Employee Assistance Professionals* (hereinafter the *Standards*) we find EAPA still talking about the "integrated model" in that same nervous, defensive, and ambivalent tone. Consider the following from the *Standards,* under the heading of:

B. Integrated Employee Assistance Program and Managed Care Systems

Standard:

The employee assistance program shall collaborate with all managed behavioral health care (MBHC) systems which provide services to the organization to establish and define the relationship between the employee assistance program and MBHC systems, and to delineate their respective roles and responsibilities.

Intent:

The role difference between EAPs and managed care organizations (MCOs) must be clearly distinguished for the organization and its employees. The primary focus of the EAP in an integrated model is the relationship between the EAP and the workplace. The primary focus of the MCO in an integrated model is the relationship between the MCO and the treatment provider. (24–25)

The only phrase I can think of to describe the content of these two passages is "intellectual schizophrenia." Despite the talk about an "integrated model," the effort throughout these two passages is to put as much distance as possible between employee assistance and managed behavioral health care. If they are "integrated," why "delineate their respective roles and responsibilities"? If they are integrated, why insist that "[t]he role difference between EAPs and managed care organizations . . . must be clearly distinguished for the organization and its employees"? If they are integrated, why state that the "primary focus of the EAP in an integrated model is the relationship between the EAP and the workplace," and the "primary focus of the MCO in an integrated model is the relationship between the MCO and the treatment provider"? Integration would suggest the existence of another entity different qualitatively from the entities that were integrated. What these two passages describe is not an integrated model but two essentially different programs existing side by side in the same arena. Their foci are different, their principles and practice are different, and their relationships are different. These two passages speak as well as anything can to the fundamental and irreconcilable differences between employee assistance and managed mental health care. And they also speak as well as anything can to the fact that what EAPA is desperately trying to do is develop some kind of rationale for coexisting with managed mental health care. We are not talking here about integration but an effort at self-preservation. There is a profound irony here: If what the authors of the *Standards* intended in these passages was to describe an integrated program, that is, a program that is some combination of managed mental health care and employee assistance, they succeeded only in suggesting the opposite.

The masquerade doesn't stop there. Consider the following, also from the *Standards:*

Essential Components:

1. The EAP must strive to establish and maintain a constructive working relationship with MBHC systems serving the organization to facilitate employees' ability to access needed treatment services.
2. The EAP must assist the organization in defining the distinction between EAP roles and responsibilities and MBHC roles and responsibilities and must assist in communicating that information to employees and organization leadership.

3. The EAP must consult with the organization regarding the planning, implementation and maintenance of MBHC benefits.

4. The EAP must serve as the primary resource for consultation to the MBHC systems and the organization on such issues as reintegration to the workplace following treatment, reasonable accommodation for behavioral health problems, and follow-up of job performance based referrals.

5. The EAP must maintain a working knowledge of the provider networks of all MCOs serving the organization and its employees.

These five passages are not essentially different conceptually from the two cited above; they merely recapitulate the intent and ideas in those two passages. But there is a slightly different and noteworthy emphasis in these later passages: All of them speak to an effort to make certain that the EAP in the integrated model will be, if not the dominant, at least an equal partner. Take, for example, the first passage, which speaks to the role of the EAP in "serving the organization to facilitate employees' ability to access needed treatment services"; the clear intent of this passage is to suggest that the EAP will not be merely a "gatekeeper" or a kind of rubber stamp for decisions made by the managed mental health care program, that it will in fact have a major if not a dominant role in determining who gains access to treatment and what that treatment will consist of. Again, the tone of this passage, as it is in so many other passages in the *Standards,* is defensive; the authors of the *Standards* perceive clearly the threat posed to the employee assistance program by the managed mental health care program, and their purpose is to prevent employee assistance from being swallowed up by the latter. Their efforts have proved futile.

There isn't much that can be added to what has already been said about the integrated model, but we might make two observations that, although somewhat repetitious, are significant. The first thing to note is that although the authors of the *Standards* seem to put their imprimatur on the integrated model, they also go to great lengths to make certain that organizations and employees understand the difference between employee assistance and managed mental health care. Every item under Intent and Essential Components addresses these differences in one way or another. Again, what we find is a great deal of ambivalence: On the one hand, the authors of the *Standards* explicitly endorse the integrated model but, on the other, strive mightily to distinguish between and separate the two programs. Why, if there is some kind of "fit" between the two programs, speak of integration and "defining" distinctions at one and the same time.

The second thing of note in the passages cited above is the assumption, implicit but nevertheless clear, that the EAP will or should be an equal, if not the dominant, partner in the integrated model. Phrases such as "must strive," "must assist," "must consult," "must serve," and "must maintain"—all with reference to the relationship between employee assistance and managed mental health care—would suggest that the authors of the *Standards,* although they have reluctantly voiced acceptance of the integrated model, are not at all comfortable with it and are making every effort not only to maintain a separate identity for employee assistance but to provide a rationale for an equal if not a dominant role. As I noted above, their stance is schizophrenia-like and ultimately futile.

Perhaps the best short critique of managed mental health care and the alliance between it and employee assistance is to be found in the July/August 1988 issue of the *EAP Digest* in an essay by George Watkins, editor in chief.

Here is some of what he had to say: "The danger of managed care is not payment accountability, utilization review, or cost control. Rather, the danger lies in taking a microeconomic view by limiting access and benefit coverage" (6). In one short succinct sentence Watkins goes right to the heart of the matter when he states that the purpose of managed mental health care is to reduce costs by "limiting access and benefit coverage." Thus the ultimate criterion of managed mental health care is cost, not care, and managed mental health care programs will be successful to the extent that they can deny or restrict access to services. Indeed, since their only purpose is to reduce costs, this is the only way in which they can be successful. Watkins continues: "We should instead regard health care expenditures as an investment in our future, not as costs." This would be to look for cost savings in the long term, a perspective that would contemplate not only greater productivity but an awareness of the exorbitant long-term costs of not treating chronic illnesses such as substance abuse and severe emotional problems. But the nature of managed mental health care precludes any such long-term view.

In the next paragraph, Watkins expands on these ideas. "In our rush to contain the costs of mental health and substance abuse care, we may be overlooking the very foundation on which the employee assistance field was built. We seem to have lost our perspective on the tremendous indirect economic costs of personal problems not only on the health care delivery system, but also on the productivity of our workforce. . . . We have long been aware of the massive indirect economic costs associated with not treating substance abuse problems—costs that result from the loss of production, motor vehicle accidents, violent crime, fire losses, disability, and premature death." Perhaps it is the nature of human nature that encourages us to look only at the present and hope that the future will take care of itself, but for society as a whole and the corporate world in particular, such a view can only portend bigger and more intractable problems and increased costs. This is axiomatic.

Finally, Watkins points to the fundamental premise of employee assistance—its emphasis on cost containment as a by-product, not a goal, of resolving problem situations in the workplace. "Today these hidden indirect costs are sometimes being overlooked because the economic connection to the corporate world is not always clear. The result is that we tend to underinvest in the care of employees with mental health or substance abuse problems when we focus on the direct costs of treatment. . . . *Cost containment should not be a goal, but a byproduct;* otherwise we become penny-wise and pound-foolish" (italics added). Watkins's words are as true today as when they were first written in 1988. Unfortunately, they were not heeded then, and they are not being heeded now.

Chapter 7

"SUPER" EAPs

Another issue that has been causing some debate in and around employee assistance circles is that of "super" EAPs, employee assistance programs that stretch the traditional boundaries of employee assistance and in some instances go beyond them. And everyone, it seems, has ideas, suggestions, recommendations, and advice for employee assistance about how it can extend its domain and at the same time become more effective. A recent issue of the *Exchange* (March/April 2001) has four articles purporting to show how "EAPs Can Provide a Sense of Community" (12), how "EAPs Can Play a Preventive Role" (14) in the area of occupational health, how there is "A New Opportunity for EAPs" (16) in promoting health and productivity, and how "EAPs Can Help Keep Workers Healthy" (19) by promoting disease prevention. Although all of the articles contain some sound ideas and principles, there is more than a little irony here; at a time when employee assistance is in a state of dissolution, or, what is the same thing, when it is merely one component of a hybrid, it is being asked to do those things that only an intact and principled agent can do. The less employee assistance resembles employee assistance, the more it is being asked to do as employee assistance. This is merely one more indication of the confusion present in the field today. And, once again, we are confronted with demands for change. Based on the proposition that the changes and upheavals in American society over the past several decades have challenged institutions of all kinds, critics suggest that those institutions, in one way or another, will have to come to terms with the new reality implicit in those challenges. And, some suggest, employee assistance is no exception. Writing in the June 1991 issue of the *Exchange*, Bradley Googins has the following to say about change and employee assistance: "The EAP field today is confronted with new realities which bring the EAP into contact with broader macro-forces. The once stable world of American business and industry is now caught up in a vortex of social, economic, and political forces. The work-place within which EAPs operate continues to undergo dramatic trans-formations, both in terms of its external environment (e.g., global competition, trade issues, growing federal and state deficits) and its in-ternal environment (e.g., downsizing, focus on quality, shifting demo-graphics). As EAPs begin to understand these changing forces and how they impact EAP practice, they are forced to reexamine EAP dogma, core technology and longstanding assumptions which lie at the heart of EAP practice" (14). The sentiments expressed in this passage have been fairly standard fare in the employee assistance literature of the past de-cade or so. Indeed, it is hard not to find statements of this kind in the literature, but the problem again is knowing what to make of them and how to respond to them. The major theme of this passage, obviously, is change, and the subsidiary theme that of the necessity of corresponding change in employee assistance if it is to remain relevant. Beyond that, however, it is difficult to know what Googins has in mind. Neither in the passage cited or in the article as a whole is there any indication or suggestion as to how "global competition," for example, will affect em-ployee assistance or how employee assistance should respond. How, spe-cifically and concretely, should employee assistance respond to all of the changes mentioned by Googins? More to the point, perhaps, why should employee assistance reexamine its "dogma," its "core technology," and its "longstanding assumptions"? Neither logically nor empirically does Googins demonstrate any connection, or any link, or any tie whatsoever, between all the changes he mentions and the dogma, Core Technology, and longstanding assumptions of employee assistance.

What we have here again is incantation: Mention the word "change," and we get a vision of a flurry of motion and activity (accompanied by a great deal of hyperbole, "a vortex of social, economic, and political forces") that, by implication at least, is compelling and to which we have no choice but to respond with more change. But both the process and the argument are circular. The fact is that motion and activity are not necessarily synonyms for change; more likely, they are merely motion and activity.

When we talk about change in any fundamental sense, we are talking about a transformation in the *essential* nature of something. Among the definitions of essential in the *OED* are the following: "Absolutely indispensable or necessary," "Constituting or forming part of a thing's essence," and "fundamental to its composition." Similarly, the word *essence is defined* as "the intrinsic nature or character of something; that which makes it what it is . . . that something must have for it not to be something else." It's obvious from these few definitions that when Googins talks about, for example, global competition, presumably as distinct from domestic competition, there is no essential change in the nature of competition. Competition remains competition; in this case, there is merely an extension in space. This is true also of all the other "macroforces" Googins mentions. Put another way: Despite all of the activity and motion suggested by Googins, the essential nature of the corporation and the worksite remain the same; the corporation and the worksite may be larger or smaller in size, foreign or domestic, and more culturally diverse, but the corporation remains a corporation and the worksite a worksite.

All of this may seem to be no more than an exercise in belaboring the obvious, or even trivial, but it is important to emphasize and reemphasize lest we are tempted to change employee assistance in such a way that it is no longer employee assistance. When we use the word "change," we must determine whether what we are talking about is in fact change or merely motion and activity. Does the change we are talking about entail the alteration or elimination of something substantive or essential—that is, something intrinsic to or inherent in the object or entity—or merely something attributional? It is important to be clear in our own minds about what we mean when we use particular words and phrases.

We see the same kind of process at work within the Employee Assistance Professionals Association. In the *Standards*, under Section D, "Additional Services," we find this statement: "The employee assistance program shall remain alert for emerging needs and may add new services when they are consistent with and complementary to the employee assistance program (EAP) core technology" (4). The next paragraph includes the following: "Services to meet these [emerging] needs may be incorporated into the EAP as long as they do not reduce the effectiveness or perceived neutrality of the EA professional and program." Still further down on the same page we encounter the following, under the heading of Essential Component: "When considering the addition of any new services, the EAP must first determine that the new services are consistent with and will not damage the core EAP functions, goals, and objectives." Finally, under the heading of Examples, there is this: "EAP staff and organization leadership analyze and attempt to predict the impact that the new role will have on both supervisory and self-referrals, employee perception of the EA professional and/or program, and the resources of the EAP. If there is no predicted negative effect, the new role is added."

As we will see shortly, none of this makes much sense; the notion of "new services" seems to have been concocted in a vacuum. There is neither an explanation, or, more precisely, a rationale for something called "new services," nor is there an end or purpose, which is to say, we are not told, at least in the *Standards,* how these new services enhance or contribute to the purposes of employee assistance. The notion of new services simply appears, seemingly out of nowhere, and, other than the fact that the phrase appears in the *Standards,* we are not told what these new services are.

In 1998 EAPA released an illustration listing the elements of the Core Technology, those items included in the category of "EAP-related services," and indicating the relationship of employee assistance to managed care services. Included under the heading of EAP-related services are the following: the Family/Medical Leave Act, Child/Elder Care Services, Legal/Financial referral, Outplacement/Retirement, Welfare-to-Work Programs, Americans with Disabilities Act Teams, Conflict Management/ Violence Prevention/Threat Assessment Teams, Drug Free Workplace, OSHA/Safety Programs, Wellness Promotion, Disability Management, Work/Life Programs, Critical Incident/Stress Management, Return-to-Duty Assistance, Support Groups, Risk Management, and Substance Abuse Professional Services.

First of all, it is not clear what "EAP-related" means. Does it mean that the services cited above are legitimate EAP functions? If so, how was that legitimacy determined? What was EAPA's purpose in describing these services as "EAP-related"? Is the purpose to encourage employee assistance professionals to take on additional responsibilities? At the very least, the notion of EAP-related services is murky. Secondly, it may very well be that several of the services listed above (for example, risk management) are legitimate functions for EAP programs, but there are others (for example, OSHA/Safety Programs), which are doubtful candidates for inclusion. But whether any or all of these are legitimate candidates for inclusion really begs a prior and, indeed, the important question: What is the criterion or criteria by which the services listed above are included within the range of EAP services, presuming that was EAPA's intention in describing these services as EAP-related? The *Standards* speaks of consistency and complementarity and "no predicted negative effects" but are these criteria? It is impossible to determine, at least from the *Standards,* what EAP-related means, or what "consistent with" and "complementary to" mean, or how and why EAPA decided to include whole new categories of services within the range of EAP activities. It should be kept in mind that institutions come into existence to serve a limited and specific purpose, and to the degree that they serve that purpose they are usually successful. When, however, they presume to take on a variety of purposes they become increasingly vulnerable to becoming "jacks of all trades and masters of none." As I noted earlier, our public schools today are a perfect illustration of that old adage.

The fact is that one will look in vain in the *Standards* or in any other piece of literature published by EAPA for any criterion or criteria that might be helpful in determining what "EAP-related" means or which "new" or "related" services merit inclusion in the field of employee assistance. "Consistent with" and "complementary to" are not criteria; they are what might be called propositions in that they merely assert or claim that the service under consideration possesses some affinity with, similarity to, or capacity for, integration with employee assistance as the latter is defined by the Core Technology. They do not tell us how or why the service should be included or how it is related.

And when EAPA suggests the following—"do not reduce the effectiveness or perceived neutrality of the EA professional and program," "will not change the core EAP functions," and "no predicted negative effects"—as criteria, and I'm presuming that these are intended as criteria, it raises the obvious question: What could not be included within the range of EAP activities under these criteria? Or when the *Standards* suggests that "EAP staff and organization leadership analyze and attempt to predict the impact" of the proposed new service, we are again confronted with an obvious question: How does one "predict the impact"? Then there is what appears to be a contradiction: On the one hand, the *Standards* suggests that "consistent with" and "complementary to" are criteria for evaluating the appropriateness of new services for inclusion within the range of EAP services, and, on the other, that "do not reduce the effectiveness," "will not damage," and "no predicted negative effects," are also criteria for doing the same thing. The problem is that these two sets of criteria easily cancel one another out. To state that something must be "consistent with" or "complementary to" is to state that the thing being considered for inclusion must possess some qualification or attribute that could make it a candidate for inclusion. But to state, for example, that the thing being considered for inclusion "will not damage the core EAP functions" as a criterion is to say no more than that the thing being considered for inclusion not be harmful to the inclusive entity. In the first instance, that of consistency and complementarity, we are at least demanding that the thing under consideration for inclusion possess some qualification or characteristic that would make it eligible for consideration, that is, we are trying to determine whether the thing under consideration for inclusion possesses qualities or attributes that would enhance or improve the ability of the inclusive entity to achieve its end or purpose, and if it would how it would. In the case of the negative criteria, however, we are stating, implicitly at least, that the thing being considered for inclusion need not possess any of those necessary characteristics and that the only thing necessary is that it not do any harm. It's difficult to know what the authors of the *Standards* had in mind when they wrote the latter. Why did they decide that the profession needed to incorporate or align itself with new and/or EAP-related services, and what was the ground of their decision? Again, what does "EAP-related services" mean?

Here the confusion in the *Standards* as to what constitutes and what does not constitute a legitimate EAP function is apparent, and in turn the confusion throughout the profession about the nature and purpose of employee assistance has its source in the confusion in the ranks of the leadership. When we speak of the Core Technology, the operative word is "core," and the word itself presumes the essential or foundational nature of the entity and the extent of its boundaries. In other words, it has a beginning and an end.

One has to wonder if there isn't a degree of hubris combined with an element of fear in the efforts of many employee assistance professionals to be all things to all people. Writing in the September/October 1996 issue of *Employee Assistance* ("'Super' Profession or Virtual Value," 4), Carole McMichael makes some interesting observations and asks some pertinent questions about what seems to be a growing trend towards super EAPs: "Many EA professionals are pressured to be experts in every kind of problem-solving that affects workplace behavior or job performance: making optimum clinical referrals; covering all the bases from discrimination to work/family to risk management; cleaning up after downsizing debacles; preventing their own burnout; and most especially, proving their dollar-and-cents worth." McMichael's observations are accurate, and they raise a singularly important question: Why have employee assistance professionals capitulated to the demand that they provide a kind of all-purpose service? To put the question another way: What is it about the profession, or its structure, or its present principles

and practice, which inhibits or discourages efforts to set limits or establish boundaries? Again, why is the profession unable to articulate a co-
herent and systematic set of first principles that would be clear to all and
that would establish firmly and lastingly what an employee assistance
program is and what it is not? (We will attempt in the Conclusion to
provide at least tentative and preliminary answers to these questions.)

McMichael also draws an interesting and instructive parallel between
the employee assistance profession and the medical profession, especially
those in the medical profession who are under contract to managed care
programs. "Even though EAs will probably bow to the pressure to perform as Super EAPs as a business expediency, they should consider what
has happened to many primary care doctors. Managed care has empow-
ered them to make referrals for problems that often require the diagnos-
ing expertise of specialists but without their training and given them a
lot of incentive to keep the sessions short." McMichael's point here is
crucial to understanding what is happening in many employee assistance
programs; because they are unable or unwilling to establish firm boundaries, which is to say, unable or unwilling to state and enforce with any
conviction the essential principles of employee assistance, they are performing functions for which they are poorly trained or performing so
many functions that they do few or none of them well. Indeed, this
inability to say no and its unfortunate consequences are two of the major
reasons why managed mental health care programs have been able to
assume control of the employee assistance field. Managed mental health
care is not the source of the profession's difficulties; it is merely the
effect.

Finally, McMichael raises two important questions that, she believes,
those in the profession should ask themselves: "How fast can a service
be performed and still be effective? How thin can expertise be spread
before it becomes an illusion?" Unfortunately, McMichael's comments
and questions are seldom addressed in the literature. But we need to ask:
What are the criteria or standards, if any, for determining which institutional activities are consistent with and complementary to the Core
Technology? What would be the principle or axiom, if there is one, from
which we could deduce those criteria or standards? Once we ask these
questions, we bracket, at least temporarily, the concept of change or,
more specifically, the concept of change as a criterion or standard. Put
another way: We need to spend less time making hyperbolic statements
about change and entertaining grandiose ideas about strategic alliances
and more time developing criteria or standards to determine what does
and what does not belong under the canopy of employee assistance.

More specifically, what is that principle or principles on the basis of which we can develop a criterion or criteria to determine those activities that could legitimately come under the heading of employee assistance? Is there anything in the history and experience of employee assistance, or in the standard definition of employee assistance, or in the Core Technology, which might provide us with some direction? Once we ask these questions, we are back once again where we began—in the worksite. This, and not managed mental health care or the therapist's office or EAP-related services, is the indispensable starting point, and once we focus on the worksite and its dynamics, we have begun to identify core functions and establish boundaries. And here the *Standards* (v) are helpful. First—at the risk of some repetition—the definition of employee assistance as it is written in the *Standards,* followed by the preamble to the Core Technology and the first item in the Core Technology:

> "Employee Assistance Program" or "EAP" is a worksite-based program designed to assist (1) work organizations in addressing productivity issues, and (2) "employee clients" in identifying and resolving personal concerns, including, but not limited to, health, marital, family, financial, alcohol, drug, legal, emotional, stress, or other personal issues that may affect job performance.

Now the preamble to the Core Technology and the first item in the Core Technology:

> "Employee Assistance Program core technology" or "EAP core technology" represents the essential components of the employee assistance (EA) profession. These components combine to create a unique approach to addressing work-organization productivity issues and "employee client" personal concerns affecting job performance and ability to perform on the job. EAP core technology is
>
> (1) Consultation with, training of, and assistance to work organization leadership (managers, supervisors, and union stewards) seeking to manage the troubled employee, enhance the work environment, and improve employee job performance; and, outreach to and education of employees and their family members about availability of EAP services [.]

The first thing to note are the words "worksite-based program," "productivity issues," and "personal issues that may affect job performance" in the definition of employee assistance. These appear before the preamble and the several items in the Core Technology and establish the context or the boundaries for that which we call employee assistance. It is the worksite and its dynamics—productivity, the troubled employee, and the work environment—that constitute the conceptual framework for and dictate the activities of employee assistance professionals. The second thing to note is the line in the preamble that defines the Core Technology as "the *essential*" components of the employee assistance (EA) profession" (italics added). The next line reads: "These components combine to create a *unique* approach to addressing work-organization productivity issues and 'employee client' personal concerns affecting job performance and ability to perform on the job" (italics added). If the definition gives us the context or the boundaries within which the employee assistance consultant does his work, the Core Technology provides him with the tools and guidelines to accomplish his tasks. This is essentially no different from any other profession that will also have its boundaries and a "Core Technology" that spells out what is to be done and how it is to be done. Finally, there are the words "troubled employee" and "improve employee job performance" in the first item of the Core Technology; they tell us clearly who the subject of the professional's efforts is—the employee whose job performance is not satisfactory and who is creating difficulties for himself, his colleagues, and the work organization.

Although all of this may seem a bit repetitious, it is, I believe, necessary to emphasize and reemphasize the fact that employee assistance is circumscribed by the worksite and its dynamics and that the Core Technology prescribes precisely the structure and purpose of the profession. All of this would not have to be said were it not for the fact that the Core Technology is more often than not conspicuous by its absence in many programs that call themselves employee assistance programs.

Collectively, the definition of employee assistance, the preamble to the Core Technology, and the Core Technology itself constitute the first principle of employee assistance, that which makes employee assistance employee assistance and without which employee assistance is not employee assistance; these, in other words, constitute the ground or foundation of employee assistance, and it was designed, as the preamble states, as "a unique approach to addressing work-organization productivity issues and 'employee client' personal concerns affecting job performance and ability to perform on the job." Thus it is the troubled employee, that is, the employee whose personal concerns are adversely affecting his job performance, who is the subject of the Core Technology, which is to say, employee assistance. Perhaps another way of saying this is that the Core Technology not only represents the core of employee assistance but also establishes clear and definite boundaries for the profession. All of these words and phrases—"troubled employee," "productivity issues," "resolving personal problems . . . that may affect job performance" "ability to perform on the job," and "improve employee job performance"—suggest the same thing, namely, that it is the troubled employee, the employee whose job performance is not adequate and who is consequently a source of concern for management as well as coworkers, who is or should be the focus of employee assistance.

If this is the case, if in fact the purpose of employee assistance is to manage the troubled employee, that is, the employee whose job performance is not satisfactory, then several questions relative to the notion of super EAPs are in order. Is the employee who is seeking time off under FMLA but whose job performance is adequate "troubled"? What about the employee who is retiring, or the employee who is in a welfare-to-work program, or who comes under the provisions of the ADA? Is he "troubled"? Moreover, how, specifically, do OSHA and safety programs, wellness promotion, disability management, work/life programs, return-to-duty assistance, and support groups relate to or encompass the "troubled employee"? Are employees who have any kind of connection—however tentative or tenuous—to these programs "troubled"? If they are, then we can only conclude that the definition of "troubled" has been expanded to include people who have concerns of any kind—which is everyone. This is a little like the present *Diagnostic and Statistical Manual of Mental Disorders IV (DSM IV)*, which continues to manufacture whole new classes of mental illness and whose definitions of the latter are so broad and whose criteria for determining mental illness are so loose that everyone, without exception, would come under one or more categories in the manual.

Here we are face-to-face with a phenomenon peculiar to our age—the inflation of language. If the "troubled employee," within the context of an expanded definition of what constitutes employee assistance, means no more than the "concerned employee," then employee assistance is indeed faced with a dilemma, for if everyone is troubled then no one is troubled, hence there cannot be, nor need there be, criteria for distinguishing one thing from another. And this inability or unwillingness to develop criteria, to make distinctions, to discriminate, is exactly what led to the demise of the codependency movement. When several of its leading theorists pronounced everyone as codependent, the movement expired.

There are additional problems with the notion of "EAP-related" services. Given the expansionist tendencies of some employee assistance programs and EAPA's interest in "strategic alliances," a legitimate question is: Is the field as a whole engaged in empire building? Also, is employee assistance encroaching on areas traditionally the province of other departments or units or programs, such as, for example, human resources, which usually encompasses such areas as FMLA, ADA, and termination and retirement? Do employee assistance professionals have the expertise to become involved in areas such as these?

It is, I suppose, flattering to be asked by employers to take on additional responsibilities in an era when complexity seems to increase at an exponential rate. But it is important to keep in mind that one cannot discard that which is essential to a principle, that which makes a principle that principle and no other, and still retain the principle. Perhaps another way of saying this is that it is incumbent upon employee assistance practitioners to distinguish between what is substantive about employee assistance, which is to say, that which defines its core and marks off its boundaries, and that which is merely peripheral. To say this is not to suggest that employee assistance should not function in a cooperative way with other departments, such as human resources, workmen's compensation, or disability management. It is, rather, to suggest that some degree of humility is essential for individual EAP practitioners and for the profession as a whole.

CONCLUSION: FUNCTION AND AUTHORITY

Just a few days ago, when I was listening to the morning news on one of our local television stations, I learned that there is now a college in the United States offering a bachelor's degree in astrology. I was not at all surprised, since it was just a few months ago when I learned that another college is offering course credit to those who would like to study the Klingon language. And I would be willing to bet that there are still other institutions of higher learning offering degrees or course credit for similar kinds of studies.

Some might argue that there is nothing wrong with this, that all subjects are of equal value, or that people have the right to spend their money on whatever catches their fancy, or that this is just all harmless fun. But whatever the rationale, one thing is certain: Bachelor's degrees in astrology and course credit for studying a nonexistent language, although perhaps humorous at first glance, are symptomatic of a fundamental malaise in our culture. We have lost the ability to say no, and it is precisely this inability to say no that is at the root of so many of our problems. For if we cannot say no then everything, every idea, notion, whim, and hallucination—however contradictory, nonsensical, or repugnant to common sense—must be admitted to the realm of discourse on an equal basis and without qualification. At the very least, the result of our inability to say no leaves us very vulnerable to the manipulations of the unscrupulous ideologue who comes armed with absolute certainty and the promise of utopia. Just a cursory review of all of the "isms" and movements in our society today would be sufficient proof of that assertion. The upshot is that we cannot mention the word "truth," even truth with a small "t", without being subject to ridicule. The word itself, it seems, no longer has an honored place in our lexicon.

In a brilliant article entitled "The Nemesis of Authority," in *Encounter* magazine for August 1972, Robert Nisbet paints a vivid and accurate portrait of the state of our culture. "Revolt against authority has already reached a higher point than in any other period in the West since perhaps the final years of the Roman Empire. Apart from this revolt it is impossible, I believe, to understand the spreading 'failure of nerve,' the widening cultural sterility, the general spirit of absurdity and degradation that characterizes so much of what is called the arts at the present time. If it were revolt solely against Government, or against war, or against the Economy, the problem would not be acute, at least in our large, diverse, and plural society. It is, however, revolt against any and all forms of authority, even those which manifest themselves as the simplest of techniques in the arts, the most elemental canons of judgment" (11–12).

Nisbet's depiction of the state of our culture is accurate; indeed, it may even be worse today than it was in 1972 when Nisbet wrote his article. Certainly, the "failure of nerve" (and this is very descriptive of employee assistance today) is more widespread than it ever has been. We see this in efforts to accommodate every kind of speech or behavior, no matter how bizarre, from interviews with incoherent rap "musicians" to inviting convicted murderers to deliver commencement addresses at university graduation ceremonies. Nothing, it seems, can be excluded from the realm of discourse. But, as Nisbet suggests, even this is prologue. "When revolt against all ordinary, traditional authorities had worn itself out, had become the object of boredom, there was nothing left but revolt against even the idea of revolt, and the results are to be seen in worship of the absurd, in consecration of the trivial and the inane, and in a state of language and culture that leaves psychedelic experience almost the only way out." Nisbet's words may be harsh, but they ring true. Is it any wonder that astrology and a nonexistent language have made their debut? But we are left with a question: What is "the nemesis of authority," which is the theme of Nisbet's article? The answer is power—raw unrestrained power that knows no limits, has nothing but contempt for tradition and authority, and seeks to reconstitute the social order along ideological lines. Again, Nisbet: "It is impossible to miss among the selfsame intellectuals who have made destruction of traditional authority their sovereign aim a fascination with the kind of power that is inseparable from social movements and crusades. . . . Such power gives the illusion of being based in 'the people,' of being redemptive and avenging at one and the same time, of proffering community, and of rescuing the alienated and anomic from the boredom and corruptions of ordinary existence" (19). Although Nisbet's focus here is on intellectuals and their fascination with power, he is well aware that power is very capable of slipping the leash of restraint in an infinite variety of ways and manifesting itself in the ordinary and the mundane, and that given the opportunity power will seek to demolish any and every form of authority. We see this in institutions and communities of every kind, in academic settings, in corporations, and in government at all levels. Power is the deadly enemy of authority. The history of the twentieth century is sufficient proof of that assertion.

We are still, however, left with a question: If power is the nemesis of authority, what is the nature of authority and how does it act to restrain power? And again Nisbet provides us with an answer. "Authority, unlike power or coercion, is not rooted in force, or threat of force. It is built into the very fabric of human association. Authority exists in the very roles and statuses of the social order. It is no more than an aspect, though a vital aspect, of the social bond. It is closely related to function, to membership, and to allegiance, in any degree whatever. In any reasonably stable community or association, function, authority, and membership form a seamless web. Freedom, in any positive, creative sense, is inseparable from a structure of authority—of rules, norms, roles, and statuses—which can alone give the stamp of character to the free mind" (11). What Nisbet is suggesting here is that authority is not monolithic, as is power, but is rather plural in nature and defined by the roles and statuses attributed to individuals and associations in their various communities. And because it is plural in nature and "built into the very fabric of human association," which is to say, it has a taken-for-granted quality endorsed by tradition, it is able to fragment and thus restrain power. Power is dispersed over and invested in any number of rules, norms, roles, and statuses, thus making it difficult for any single individual or institution to gain and exercise inordinate power. Perhaps another way of saying this is that in any association or community governed by legitimate power, there is a system of checks and balances wherein all of the components of the system, all of its rules, norms, roles, and statuses, act to restrain one another. Power, in other words, is restrained by power.

Unfortunately, however, this same plurality is its major weakness, for in times of stress or crisis, authority or, more precisely, that plurality of authorities, because it is discreet and divided among any number of individuals, associations, and communities, is weak and ineffectual and can be induced to give way to "the man on the white horse" who promises succor and relief for the distressed but only if all power is placed in his hands. In all too many of these instances, the cure is worse than the disease.

Moreover, unrestrained power, and this is one of its insidious aspects, likes to clothe itself in some kind of legitimacy in order to appear benign. Witness the constitution of the former Soviet Union, wherein its citizens were "guaranteed" all sorts of rights, or the People's Republic of China, wherein there is a pretense of popular sovereignty. The holders of unrestrained power know very well that the kind of power they wield is crude and menacing, and that if they are to gain the acceptance of their subject populations, they must present unrestrained power as something other than what it is. Power must be garbed in the most benign forms possible and appear to be wielded for their sake and in their interests.

Although we have been talking about the dynamics of authority and power in a very broad and abstract sense, these very same dynamics are present in the most mundane and ordinary aspects of our everyday lives. We see them, for example, in our economy, where competition among producers, distributors, and sellers acts as a restraint on monopoly, also an insidious form of power, or in the little and ultimately meaningless office power struggles where roles and statuses compete with ambition. Indeed, it is not too much to say that if authority did not exist and was not a consequence of function, we would have to invent it. For, as Nisbet reminds us: "In any reasonably stable community or association, function, authority, and membership form a seamless web." Perhaps another way of saying this is that in any reasonably stable community, authority, because it is a consequence of function, is virtually invisible. It is the function we see and honor, or at least respect. None of this is to suggest that change does not take place; it does, and in many instances it is desirable and necessary that authority be amended to accommodate changing conditions and circumstances. Authority and power are always and everywhere in a state of tension relative to each other, and it is well that they should be, but even here prudence should be our watchword.

All of this may seem like an inordinately roundabout way to address the situation of employee assistance today or no more than an exercise in rootless abstraction, but it is, I believe, entirely relevant to our discussion of the causes of the problems affecting employee assistance and the conditions in which it finds itself. If we wish to understand the present predicament of employee assistance, it is necessary to examine the intellectual and social roots of the problem, which are the very same roots affecting so many institutions in our society. The presence of astrology and a nonexistent language in the curriculum of institutions of higher learning can be traced to the very same source, and that is the relinquishing of authority. And when we relinquish authority, we can no longer say no. This is the point of Nisbet's article, and we will use his conceptual framework as our framework for the discussion that follows.

So the question is: What does all of this have to do with employee assistance? And the answer is: a great deal. Employee assistance also finds itself in the position of being unable to or unwilling to say no, and the result has been disastrous for the field. Its authority has been shattered and its membership and leadership confused as to what does and what does not constitute an employee assistance program. The Core Technology is conspicuous by its absence, many of the association's members are driven by a kind of social activism, and its leadership is making every effort to hide in the deepest recesses of a mindless abstraction.

The first mistake made by the profession was to sever its ties with the community that comprised ALMACA, for in so doing it diminished its authority. This was the first step in withdrawing from the worksite, and it proved to be the prelude to subsequent disasters. When the profession severed its ties with labor and management, it set in motion a chain of events—among them, the relativization of alcohol problems in the workplace and the role of management and labor in resolving problem situations in the workplace—that left it ineffective in the worksite, thus defenseless against the pretensions of managed mental health care that claimed to have the solution to the crisis of rapidly increasing health care costs, especially the costs of mental health care. In effect, managed mental health care was the man on the white horse; it claimed to have the techniques, all of course scientifically based, to resolve the crisis. But there was a catch—it could do so, it claimed, but only if all power over assessments, evaluations, and the determination of criteria for who would and who would not be admitted into the system were placed in its hands. This was an exercise in unrestrained power, and employee assistance, because it had relinquished its authority, could only stand by helplessly and watch whatever authority it had left quickly dissipate.

But this, as one well-known radio commentator puts it, was only part of the story. The rest of the story follows the all too familiar pattern of unrestrained power seeking some form of legitimation for its activities, and that legitimation was close at hand in the form of employee assistance. Thus, employee assistance, because it was weakened and essentially ineffectual, served the purposes of managed mental health care well, for two reasons: (1) given its weaknesses, it would not, as the proponents of managed mental health care knew, offer much resistance to the blandishments of the latter; and (2) because historically it had ties to the corporate world, it was the perfect cover for the activities of the managed mental health care industry. It was an ideal situation for the entrepreneurs who were interested in jobs and contracts and had little or no interest in what Paul Roman describes as the "resolution of a quite wide range of problem situations in the workplace." And not all the talk in the world about the integrated program being "EAP-driven" or integration strengthening employee assistance will make it otherwise.

As I noted above, the roots of the problem in employee assistance today are exactly the same as those that prompt institutions of higher education to grant bachelor's degrees in astrology and course credit for studying a nonexistent language. Our culture actively discourages the discussion, not to mention implementation, of standards, principles, or norms—in a word, authority—and seeks to deny a voice to those who insist that without criteria for making judgments and evaluating ideas a culture is moribund. Witness the extraordinary power of political correctness on our college and university campuses today to silence dissent. It is not at all coincidental that at the very same time dissent is being stifled, astrology and science fiction are coming into their own.

Where does employee assistance go from here? Since I haven't been granted the gift of prophecy, I can't say with any certainty what the future holds for the field. But given the trajectory of the profession over the past decade and a half or so and the inability or unwillingness of its practitioners and especially its leadership to safeguard its heritage, we can make some speculative and tentative comments. Given the damage done to the field, damage done entirely by employee assistance professionals themselves, it is doubtful whether the field can survive, at least not as a profession or discipline governed by principles inherent in its relationship to the worksite. Entrepreneurs and ideologues—frequently the same people—today dominate the field, and there is very little evidence that they understand the problem, or, if they do, that they have any interest in addressing it. The ends or purposes of the entrepreneurs and ideologues have little or nothing in common with the ends or purposes inherent in or intrinsic to employee assistance, at least as employee assistance is defined by the Core Technology. If it does survive, there are several things that must happen.

First, those in the field, especially the leadership, must confront their own denial about the state of employee assistance today. Instead of self-congratulatory statements about imaginary accomplishments, or grandiose conceptions of strategic alliances, or vague celebratory statements about growth and change, they must be willing to admit that there are serious problems in the field today. One would not know from reading the literature that there is any problem at all; there is an air of complete unreality about it—while the ship sinks, the passengers make merry. Thus the first step in recovery is admitting, and then accepting, the fact that there is a problem, that, in fact, and for a number of reasons, employee assistance has retreated from and abandoned the worksite, the only arena in which it has any meaning and the only arena in which it can have any meaning. It was born in the worksite, nurtured in the worksite, and received its definitive shape and form as a result of its activities in the worksite. Apart from the worksite, employee assistance has no meaning; apart from the worksite, it cannot and will not survive. It is from the objective nature of its activities in the worksite, and not from catering to the subjective and arbitrary whims of ideologues and entrepreneurs, that employee assistance developed its conceptual framework, and apart from the worksite that conceptual framework has no meaning.

Second, those in the field must recognize and relinquish the fallacy that other kinds of activities—such as clinical activities, alliances with managed mental health care programs, developing different kinds of EAP "models," and focusing on a host of peripheral activities—fall within the purview of legitimate employee assistance endeavors. These kinds of activities serve only to undercut the authority of employee assistance and insure its demise.

Third, and this is really the heart of the matter, there is a close, intimate, and inseparable relationship between *function* and *authority*. As I suggested above, institutions come into existence to accomplish well-defined and particular functions, and to the degree that they accomplish those functions they remain authoritative, which is to say, they can set standards, develop norms, and enunciate principles, and when they remain true to their purposes they retain their legitimacy, which in the end is the only compulsion necessary. Absent those functions, or when those functions are attenuated in any way, institutions lose the capacity to speak authoritatively—no one is listening. Moreover, when institutions abdicate their responsibility, the way is open for unrestrained power to make its presence felt. This is the position employee assistance is in today; having abdicated its responsibility, which is to say, its function, it also undercut its legitimacy, for legitimacy is entirely dependent on function, and when these went so did its authority. Neither the profession as a whole nor the leadership in particular is any longer able to speak authoritatively to the corporate community, the health care community, or, indeed, even to its own membership. This is the major reason why so much of the literature in the employee assistance field is marked by equivocation, rootless abstraction, and conceptual incoherence. But all of this is effect rather than cause.

The most serious consequence of the profession's abandonment of its principles and practice was to leave it defenseless against unrestrained power, and this was not long in coming in the form of managed mental health care. It is important to note at this point that managed mental health care did not create the problems plaguing employee assistance today; it, too, is effect rather than cause. But what the proponents of managed mental health care were able to do was exploit the vacuum at the heart of the profession. Knowing that managed mental health care had little going for it other than a singular and vague promise of cost-effectiveness, and knowing, furthermore, that that cost-effectiveness could only be the result of denying or restricting services, the proponents of managed mental health care sought to clothe their efforts in some semblance of legitimacy. And the vehicle for doing so was close at hand; although the profession was considerably weakened by its own ineptness, the proponents of managed mental health care saw that its heritage could still be useful. This is what the proponents of managed mental health care mean when they describe the integrated model as EAP-driven or that the integrated model will strengthen employee assistance. But in fact the opposite is the case; this is just a slightly updated version of "newspeak." Once again, we are reminded of Robert Nisbet's words: "In any reasonably stable community or association, function, authority, and membership form a seamless web." Indeed, it cannot be otherwise; if an institution is to realize the ends or purposes for which it was called into existence, function, authority, and membership *must* form a seamless web. Another way of saying this is that we will have either legitimate authority or illegitimate power; we will not have both.

In his recently published and insightful book, *The Death of Character: Moral Education in an Age Without Good or Evil*, James Davison Hunter sums up succinctly the elements of the doctrine of cheap grace: "We say we want a renewal of character in our day but we don't really know what to ask for. To have a renewal of character is to have a creedal order that constrains, limits, binds, obligates, compels. The price is too high to pay. We want character but without unyielding conviction; we want strong morality but without the emotional burden of guilt or shame; we want virtue but without particular moral justifications that invariably offend; we want good without having to name evil; we want decency without the authority to insist upon it; we want moral community without any limitations to personal freedom. In short, we want what we cannot possibly have on the terms that we want it" (xv). "[W]e want what we cannot possibly have on the terms that we want it." This is the doctrine of cheap grace—the notion that through ritual incantation, through easy slogans, and through a watery moralism stripped of any kind of sanction or particularity, we can quiet the storm in our souls. One has only to browse in the psychology/self-help section of any bookstore to know the truth of these assertions. But we cannot, as Hunter suggests, have it both ways; either we will have an authoritative order that binds, limits, constrains, obligates, and compels, or we will have an order in which unrestrained power is the arbiter. Hunter puts it this way: "Whatever benefits such a fluid and temporary moral universe may offer, they fail to lessen our dismay when we witness random and senseless violence . . . open displays of corruption . . . a flouting of basic standards of decency. . . . But why should we be surprised? When the self is stripped of moral anchoring, there is nothing to which the will is bound to submit, nothing innate to keep it in check. There is no compelling reason to be burdened by guilt . . . because *there are no inhibiting truths*. What is more, the indigenous moral institutions of our society that have long sustained those truths are fragile at best, irreparable at worst" (xiv, italics added).

As Hunter suggests, the problem is not merely an individual one; it is also a cultural and institutional one. In effect, it is a crisis of authority. For more than a generation now, there has been one assault after another on the basic institutions of our society. The family, the schools, our political and legal institutions, the arts, and even our conceptions of self, have been under a vigorous and sustained attack by those who, for one reason or another, view American society as corrupt, authoritarian, and lacking even rudimentary notions of social justice. Their vision is of a new egalitarian society where everyone will be "liberated"—however that word may be defined—from the stultifying and dead hand of the past. Their efforts have been enormously successful—there are few if any "inhibiting" truths left.

But to speak of inhibiting truths is to suggest at least three things: (1) that there is such a thing as truth; (2) that it can be known; and (3) that it should be controlling, that is, inhibiting. There are, in short, such things as right and wrong, and even the moral and intellectual relativist, although she may not openly acknowledge their reality, knows this to be the case. When we speak of truth, then, we are speaking of something that at one and the same time is both restricting and liberating, restricting in the sense that it compels us to evaluate objectively the world around us, and liberating in the sense that it frees us from the illusion that A is B and not A. But this takes effort and discipline, two commodities that are also in short supply in our society. The question then is this: How do we get from here to there, from an empty relativism to truths that can provide us with some semblance of authority and institutions that are authoritative. This is a journey we must take, for to forego it is to invite ideology, the Idea, to take control of our lives. However, like Hunter, I am not at all sanguine about the outcome.

There is more, much more, to be gleaned from Hunter's words, but that will have to be reserved for another time. Ultimately, what we are suggesting—and this is our main point—is that the only alternative to ideology is authority, and authority can be found only in tradition. Either we will have a community in which there is fairly widespread agreement on how we should live our lives together or a community that is such in name only and held together only by physical proximity and unrestrained power. We will not have both. So the question remains: What is the nature of a society that can provide a medium for the greatest possible human achievement and still maintain an ordered liberty?

Finally, I would like to say a few words about tradition, and I know of no better place to begin than with two very insightful scholars, Russell Kirk and Edward Shils. In his *Enemies of the Permanent Things: Observations of Abnormity in Literature and Politics*, Kirk provides us with some direction. The answer to the question posed above lies, he believes, in a renewed appreciation of tradition. "The endeavor of the intelligent believer in tradition is so to blend ancient usage with necessary amendment that society never is wholly old and never wholly new. He believes that tradition is a storehouse of wisdom" (181). Note that Kirk is not arguing against change; when he speaks of "necessary amendment" he is suggesting that change is not only inevitable in some instances but desirable. Some things need to be changed, but what do we change, and how do we change them?

To speak of tradition is anathema in some quarters, as is the word authority. Tradition is viewed as oppressive and reactionary, as keeping one in bondage to a dead past and absolutely useless as a guide to the present and the future. But to be guided by tradition is not to surrender one's mind to dead dogmas; it is, rather, to acquire the virtue of prudence. Prudence weights, sifts, and filters, and suggests that before we make radical changes we look to the past for guidance. For as Kirk suggests, "the only alternative to tradition is ideology" (181). These seven words encapsulate perfectly the only two alternatives we have; they suggest unequivocally that there are only two kinds of social medium—one that is based on tradition and ordered liberty and one that is based on unrestrained power. There is no "third way."

Prudence also suggests the twin notions of human finitude and limitation, and these in turn suggest the virtue of humility, all of which, like the words tradition and authority, are distasteful to the modern mind. There is no question that we have made progress, if progress is defined in technological terms only, but in other areas—especially that of how we are to live our lives together—the notion of progress is at best questionable. Unless we wish ideology to be our guide, we would be wise to consult tradition, for as Kirk reminds us, tradition contains "a body of enduring truth, the filtered wisdom of the species, the considered opinion and experiences of the many wise men who have preceded us in time: the normative consciousness" (263). And it is from this "normative consciousness" that we distill our principles and standards.

But back to our question: If change is inevitable and even necessary, what do we change and how do we change it? Discernments of this sort are akin to a high-wire balancing act and require respect and even sympathy for what it is we are thinking of changing, as well as for the entire social order. But "[t]here is," Edward Shils maintains, "something paradoxical in this proposition." In his *The Virtue of Civility*, he tells us (I apologize beforehand for this lengthy quote, but it is the best summation I've ever seen of the nature of tradition and change, thus well worth quoting) that "[t]he free society is a society in movement. Tradition incorporates and transmits sacred beliefs, it entails self-reproduction, stability between generations and across centuries. The rules of the game, in which the sacred is incorporated, are the precipitates of this tradition working on current thought and experience. The free society entails a critical independent attitude toward authority; tradition entails the acknowledgement of authority inherent in a belief or mode of action by virtue of its having been performed or observed in the past. Nonetheless, the traditional legitimization of the framework of free action is compatible with, and even necessary for, rational criticism and creative innovation. The traditional legitimization of the framework of free society requires, however, that the rational criticism and improvement of any institution at any given time be carried on in a context that is set by tradition—by a tradition sustained by laws and rules, which themselves derive their efficacy from the support they gain from this tradition. In this wise, any and every particular institution might in its turn be subjected to a far-reaching rational criticism and be amended and improved—but it can be done without harm to society only if, at any given time, much of the rest of the institutional system is accepted as legitimate. The legitimacy must flow from a general disposition to respect the order as a whole. Thus, at the moment when any component is subjected to the most thoroughgoing criticism and renovation, the legitimacy of the order of which it is a part must be affirmed" (111).

Shils's words provide, I believe, a necessary antidote to vague notions and statements about change, to change as a mantra, and to the idea that change is a synonym for progress. Moreover, what Shils is suggesting is that change, if it is to be mindful rather than mindless, must take place within a context that respects tradition, for it is only on the basis of tradition that we can make necessary changes. Thus, as paradoxical as it may seem, tradition provides the ground rules for and endorses change; perhaps another way of looking at this is to suggest that if we dismiss tradition then we have no way of knowing what to change or even what change means, and change then becomes change for its own sake, errant, purposeless, and ultimately, as Nisbet reminds us, absurd. Change, when it becomes necessary, must be deliberative, that is, based on discursive reasoning and guided by what has gone before.

When the proponents of managed mental health care boast that their integrated delivery systems are cost-effective or scientifically based and that it is market forces that drive their systems, they are offering us no more than a technique, which is the sole basis and sole justification for their systems. The technique is used to justify the systems and the systems the technique. And this is why Sharar and White will not see an ethics summit, at least not an ethics summit that is much more than talk—another version of the doctrine of cheap grace. The universe of ethical discourse and the universe of scientism are at opposite ends of the ethical or spiritual spectrum; the former knows nothing of technique and the latter nothing but.

Perhaps because I tend to be pessimistic by nature, I don't, at least at present, see the field surviving. But I can still hope, and my hope is that in the months and years ahead the profession regains its authority, but this will happen only if the leadership and the membership generally spend less time talking about change and more time exercising the virtue of prudence. The heritage of the profession is there to be reclaimed, but it can be reclaimed only if there is the knowledge and the will to do so.

BIBLIOGRAPHY

Anonymous. *Committee B Report.* Unpublished Document. Wichita, Kansas, 1997.

Blair, Brenda R. "Consultative Services: Providing Added Value to Employers," *EAP Association Exchange,* March/April 2002, 21–23.

Blanchard, Kenneth H., and Hersey, Paul. *Management of Organizational Behavior: Utilizing Human Resources.* Englewood Cliffs, NJ: Prentice Hall, 1988.

Blum, Terry C., and Roman, Paul M. "The Core Technology of Employee Assistance Programs," *The Almacan,* March 1985, 8–9, 16, 18–19.

Bridwell, Deborah, Collins, Jodie, and Levine, David. "A Quiet Revolution: The Movement of EAPs to Managed Care," *EAP Digest,* July/August 1988, 27–30.

Byers, William R., and Quinn, John C. "Alcoholism as a Major Focus of EAPs," in *The Human Resources Management Handbook: Principles and Practice of Employee Assistance Programs.* Samuel H. Klarreich, James L. Francek, and C. Eugene Moore, Eds. Westport, CT: Praeger, 1985, 370–80.

Carr, Elena Brown, and McCann, Bernie. "Reshaping EA Delivery: Small Business Challenge Tests Profession," *Employee Assistance,* March 1994, 10–18, 35.

Christie, Jeff. Letter to the Editor. "Committed to Our Core Values," *EAP Association Exchange,* March/April 2002, p. 7.

Cohen, Mark. Letter to the Editor. "Absence of Clarity," *EAP Association Exchange,* November/December 2000, p. 3.

EAP Solutions to the Employer Health Cost Crisis. Arlington, VA: The Employee Assistance Professionals Association, Inc., 1990.

EAPA Standards and Professional Guidelines for Employee Assistance Professionals, 1999 Edition. Arlington, VA: The Employee Assistance Professionals Association, Inc., 1999.

"EAPs Are *Worksite-based* Programs," *Metro/EAP News,* March, 1997, 1–3.

Ellul, Jacques. *The Technological Society.* New York: Vintage Books, 1964.

Fair, Gary E. *What an Executive Should Know About Employee Assistance Programs.* Chicago: Dartnell Press, 1989.

Farmer, Jennifer F., and Maynard, John B. "Strategies of Implementing an EAP," in *The Human Resources Management Handbook: Principles and Prac-*

tice of Employee Assistance Programs. Samuel H. Klarreich, James L. Francek, and C. Eugene Moore, Eds. Westport, CT: Praeger, 1985, 31–41.

Feerst, Dan, and Gill, Dodie. "Long-Term Survival, the Core Technology, and You," *EAP Association Exchange,* March/April 1998, 16–17, 19.

Googins, Bradley K. "Strengthening the Mission," *Employee Assistance,* July 1990, 29–30.

———. "EAPs and the Workplace Response (Work and Family)," *EAP Association Exchange,* June 1991, 14–18.

———. "Ruminations on Growth," *Employee Assistance,* April 1994, 10–12.

Hazlitt, Henry. *The Foundations of Morality.* Los Angeles: Nash Publishing, 1964.

How Employee Assistance Program (EAP) Functions/Services and Health Care (HC)/Managed Care (MC) Laws (a) Relate. The Employee Assistance Professionals Association, Inc., 1998 (One page graphic).

Hunter, James Davison. *The Death of Character: Moral Education in an Age Without Good or Evil.* New York: Basic Books, 2000.

King, Helene. "Do We Need a Commonly Accepted Definition?," *EAP Association Exchange,* March/April 2002, 29–30.

Kirk, Russell. *Enemies of the Permanent Things: Observations of Abnormity in Literature and Politics.* Peru, IL: Sherwood Sugden & Company, 1984.

Kreeft, Peter. *Back to Virtue: Traditional Moral Wisdom for Modern Moral Confusion.* San Francisco: Ignatius Press, 1992.

MacIntyre, Alasdair. *After Virtue: A Study in Moral Theory.* Second Edition. Notre Dame, IN: University of Notre Dame Press, 1984.

Manuso, James J. "Occupational Clinical Psychologist," in *The Human Resources Management Handbook: Principles and Practice of Employee Assistance Programs.* Samuel H. Klarreich, James L. Francek, and C. Eugene Moore, Eds. Westport, CT: Praeger, 1985, 155–62.

Masi, Dale A., in Herman I. Diesenhaus, "Program Standards: Can We Ever Agree?," *Employee Assistance Quarterly,* Winter 1985/86, 1–17.

———. *Evaluating Your Employee Assistance and Managed Behavioral Care Program.* Troy, MI: Performance Resource Press, Inc., 1994.

Maynard, John. "The Next 30 Years," *EAP Association Exchange,* March/April 2001, 2.

McKay, John "Mickey." "Time to Reclaim Our Profession," *EAP Association Exchange,* March/April 2002, 29.

McMichael, Carole. "'Super' Profession or Virtual Value," *Employee Assistance,* September/October 1996, 4.

Myers, Donald W. *Establishing and Building Employee Assistance Programs.* Westport, CT: Quorum Books, 1984.

"Myth No[.] 1: EAPs Are Part of the Employee Benefits Package," *Metro/EAP News,* March 1997, 1–3.

Nisbet, Robert. "The Nemesis of Authority," *Encounter,* August 1972, 11–21.

Novak, Michael. *The Spirit of Democratic Capitalism.* New York: American Enterprise Institute/Simon and Schuster Publication, 1982.

Rieff, Philip. *The Triumph of the Therapeutic: Uses of Faith After Freud.* Chicago: University of Chicago Press, 1966.

Roman, Paul M., and Trice, Harrison M. *Spirits and Demons at Work: Alcohol and Other Drugs on the Job.* Ithaca, NY: Cornell University, 1972.

———. "EAPs: Professionals or Entrepreneurs?," *Employee Assistance,* July 1990, 9–10.

———. "Workplace Due Process: The EA Contribution," *Employee Assistance,* January 1994, 17–18.

———. "All EA Functions Should Be Internal," *Employee Assistance,* March 1994, 10–11.

———. "The Importance of Communication," *Employee Assistance,* July 1994, 11–12.

———. "Drifting Toward the Future," *Employee Assistance,* February 1996, 21–22.

Satinover, Jeffrey Burke. "Jungians and Gnostics," *First Things,* October 1994, 41–48.

Sharar, David A. and White, William L. "Referrals and Ownership Structures," *EAP Association Exchange,* September/October 2001, 14–15.

———. "EAP Competence and Value," *EAP Association Exchange,* November/December 2001, 14–15.

Shils, Edward. *The Virtue of Civility: Selected Essays on Liberalism, Tradition, and Civil Society.* Steven Grosby, Ed. Indianapolis: Liberty Fund, Inc., 1997.

Sims, Lillian S. "Managed Mental Health Care: What It Is and How It Works," *EAP Digest,* July/August 1988.

Sonnenstuhl, William J., and Trice, Harrison M. *Strategies for Employee Assistance Programs: The Crucial Balance.* Ithaca, NY: Cornell University, ILR Press, School of Industrial and Labor Relations, 1986.

Sturdivant, Linda L. "Taking Concrete Steps," *EAP Association Exchange,* March/April 2001, 4–5.

Sturdivant, Linda. President of the Employee Assistance Professionals Association, Inc. Letter to "Fellow EAPA Members," September 10, 2001, 1–2.

Sugarman, Barry. "Strategies for a Divided Profession," *EAP Digest,* November/December 1995, 22–24.

Thornton, Bruce S. *Plagues of the Mind: The New Epidemic of False Knowledge.* Wilmington, DE: ISI Books, 1999.

Tisone, Carl R. "Just Another Burning Issue," *EAP Association Exchange,* February 1994, 11.

———. "Crossing the Bridge," *Employee Assistance,* June 1994, 12–17.

———. "Forward," in Dale A. Masi, *Evaluating Your Employee Assistance and Managed Behavioral Care Program.* Troy, MI: Performance Resource Press, Inc., 1994, vii–ix.

von Mises, Ludwig. *Human Action: A Treatise on Economics.* Third Revised Edition. Chicago: Contemporary Books, Inc., 1996.

Watkins, George T. "In-House," *EAP Digest,* July/August 1988, 6.

Weaver, Charles A. "Employee Assistance Programs," *The Handbook of Employee Benefits: Design, Funding, and Administration.* Jerry S. Rosenbloom, Ed. Homewood, IL: Dow Jones-Irwin, 1984, 316–54.

Weil, Simone. *The Need for Roots: Prelude to a Declaration of Duties Towards Mankind.* New York: Ark Paperbacks, 1952.

"What Are EAPs?," *EAP Association Exchange,* March/April 2002, 20.

Wright, David A. "Policy and Procedures: The Essential Elements in an EAP," in *The Human Resources Management Handbook: Principles and Practice of Employee Assistance Programs.* Samuel H. Klarreich, James L. Francek, and C. Eugene Moore, Eds. Westport, CT: Praeger, 1985, 13–23.

Yandrick, Rudy M. *Behavioral Risk Management: How to Avoid Preventable Losses from Mental Health Problems in the Workplace.* San Francisco: Jossey-Bass Publishers, 1996.

Zilbergeld, Bernie. *The Shrinking of America: Myths of Psychological Change.* Boston: Little, Brown and Company, 1983.

INDEX

About the Author

LAWRENCE P. MANNION has worked in the employee assistance field for twenty years. He is presently employed at Via Christi Regional Medical Center as an employee assistance consultant in the employee assistance program.